THE STILLBORN

THE ARAB LIST

THE STILLBORN

Notebooks of a Woman from the
Student-Movement Generation in Egypt

ARWA SALIH

TRANSLATED BY SAMAH SELIM

LONDON NEW YORK CALCUTTA

Series Editor
HOSAM ABOUL-ELA

Seagull Books, 2018

Originally published in Arabic
© Hamdy Saleh, 2018

First published in English translation by Seagull Books, 2017
English translation © Samah Selim, 2017

ISBN   978 0 8574 2 483 9

British Library Cataloguing-in-Publication Data
A catalogue record for this book is available from the British Library.

Typeset by Seagull Books, Calcutta, India
Printed and bound by Maple Press, York, Pennsylvania, USA

Contents

Translator's Introduction[1]

Arwa Salih was an Egyptian communist who came of political age in the early 1970s—in the aftermath of the Six-Day Arab–Israeli War of 1967, the end of the Nasser era and the beginning of Anwar Al-Sadat's transitional regime. She belonged to the transformative political moment instigated by the radical student movement of that decade and the political generation known as 'the generation of the seventies'. She was a member of the central committee of the Marxist–Leninist Egyptian Communist Workers Party (ECWP), the major Marxist group of the decade, and quickly acquired a reputation among her mentors and comrades as a gifted and fiery young cadre. Though she was known among her peers as a talented writer, her extant published work is scant for reasons that partly have to do with the nature of the underground political work of the times (she wrote mainly for the ECWP's paper) and the fact that she was a woman in a world of men. Apart from the this book, she published an Arabic translation of Tony Cliff's 1984 book *Class*

1 I would like to express my deep gratitude to the friends and comrades who offered invaluable ideas, assistance and support during the various stages of this project: Biju Mathew, Hassan Saber, Yasser Abdel-Latif and Magda Magdy. Special thanks go to Mohammed Ezzeldin who meticulously proofread and corrected various drafts of the manuscript.

Struggle and Women's Liberation. The only other published material available to readers is a short and hastily edited selection of her papers made in 1998, one year after her death, which includes an excerpt from her memoirs, a long poem and a study of the novelist Son'allah Ibrahim's fiction.[2]

This chequered and truncated writing career haunts Salih's poignant self-interrogations in *The Stillborn*. In fact, the entire book (written in 1991 and published with a new introduction in 1996, 25 years after the 1971–72 Tahrir Square student demonstrations that rocked the nation) is a kind of haunted house in which Salih explores the question of failure: the failure of the national liberation project, the failure of communism and of her generation's political movement, and her personal failure as the subject of a utopian history. Throughout her adult life, Salih suffered from severe clinical depression and episodes of schizophrenia. After a number of unsuccessful attempts, she committed suicide in 1997, just a few months after *The Stillborn* appeared in print.

The spectral nature of Salih's legacy refracts the broader history of the Egyptian left of her generation. Edited and published documents are few and far between, and scholarly studies of the post-1967 student

---

2 Arwa Salih, *Saratan al-Rawh* [Cancer of the Soul] (Cairo: Dar al-Nahr, 1998).

movement quite rare[3]—a state of affairs which is partly due, again, to the underground activities of the movement as a whole and its sectarian character, but also to its representing an unfinished, or 'stillborn', historical project. To this day, it remains a contentious, fragmented and unofficial or secret history: a bricolage of stray documents, oral archive, memoir and occasional essay, not to mention ongoing polemical and personal enmities. Its status as unfinished history is also why it poses a series of urgent and seminal questions to today's post-2011 moment. Salih's book—the questions it elicits, the critique it constructs and the history of failure that it proposes—returns to haunt the generation that gathered in the same iconic Liberation Square to make the revolution of 2011.

The book excited much controversy—scandal even—when it was first published. It went out of print soon after Salih's death and the press itself closed down. Almost 20 years later, in 2016, it was reissued by the Egyptian General Book Organization, a Ministry of Culture organ, as part of its popular and cheaply priced 'family library' series. The irony of this fact is

---

3 See Ahmed Abdalla, *The Student Movement and National Politics in Egypt, 1923–1973* (Cairo: American University in Cairo Press, 2008). Abdalla was one of the leaders of the 1970s student movement, and the book is based on his Cambridge University PhD thesis. See also Gennaro Gervasio's excellent PhD dissertation: 'Intellectuals and Marxism in Egypt: A History of the Secular Opposition, 1967–1981' (Istituto Universitario Orientale, Naples, 1998), published in 2010 in Arabic translation.

remarkable, but so is the timing of the book's repub-
lication: three years after yet another grand failure in
the history of the Egyptian left which witnessed an
unprecedented state massacre of civilians, a massive
wave of detentions and arrests, a complete shutdown
of public space and discourse and breakdown of the
rule of law, an open geopolitical alliance with Israel
and a rush to full integration into the neoliberal
market regime of the IMF and World Bank. And yet,
in spite of this official 20-year disappearance, Salih
and her book never went away. Both the woman and
her razor-sharp critique of her generation of intellectuals and militants remained a constant, subterranean
presence in the political imagination and the recrimi-
nations, polemics and debates of those 20 intervening
years.

The Stillborn is impossible to classify in terms of form
and genre, a fact that Salih herself alludes to in the
1996 introduction. It is not memoir, though experience and memory are at the core of its form and critical project. It is not history, though every sentence,
every instance of analysis and critique is imbued with
historical knowing. And finally, it is not an essay in
political economy or sociology, though one of the main
strands of the book is a coherent class- and gender-
based analysis of the failure of both the national liberation and the Marxist projects in Egypt. It is none of

these things and all of these things. Salih's critics, of course, used the fact of the book's wayward and polyphonic modality against her. But the book's complex and shifting modal form can be read as a rich instantiation of a gendered epistemological project, one in which a biopolitics of experiencing, knowing and feeling become the bedrocks of self-interrogation, social analysis and political critique.

The transformative 10 years between 1967 and 1977 form the historical background of Salih's analysis. The stunning Egyptian defeat in the Six-Day War and Israel's occupation of the Sinai Peninsula was a devastating blow to the Egyptian 'revolutionary' order of the 1952 regime, and to Arab nationalism as well as the Palestinian national struggle. But it also opened a window for grassroots popular mobilizations in a political space that had been co-opted and monopolized by the Gamel Abdel Nasser regime for almost two decades. Student and worker strikes proliferated; there was an explosion of open and impassioned political debate in the press and a creative burst in all kinds of cultural expression. Nasser's sudden death in 1970 and his replacement by Anwar al-Sadat took place against the background of the continuing occupation of Egyptian lands. In 1971, Sadat's purge of communists and Nasserist cadres and officials, and his 'corrective revolution', sparked a realignment of the old left and a breakdown of the populist 'social compact' of the Nasser era.

The student movement of the 1970s was born in this transitional moment, the movement of a generation who had come of age in 1967, who had no history of accommodation with the regime and for whom the most urgent issue was the liberation of Sinai and the national struggle against US imperialism. The demonstrations and strikes of 1972–73 were organized around the demand that Egypt go to war to reclaim its sovereign territory and challenge Israeli—and by extension US—imperial designs in the region. Student strikes and protests through the first months of 1972 galvanized public opinion and mobilized a wider popular movement. In the face of this unrest, Sadat, who had yet to establish a basis for his legitimacy as Nasser's successor, relied on a strategy of deferral: 'the state of not-war and not-peace'. The regime stuttered and stalled in the face of the popular challenge to its legitimacy while cracking down ferociously on the universities. Hundreds of student activists were arrested and detained and many were tried and sentenced on trumped-up charges.

But the strikes and demonstrations continued unabated throughout 1973 and spilt out of university campuses onto Egypt's streets, squares and factories. Sadat's surprise military campaign against Israeli occupation in October 1973—the Yom Kippur War or October War—was as sudden as it was effective as far as the domestic situation was concerned. The stunningly successful crossing of the Suez Canal by Egyptian ground forces and their rapid advance to the strategic Sinai passes made Sadat an instant national hero and gave his regime the legitimacy it had lacked. Sadat used his new position to negotiate an abject ceasefire with Israel, consolidate his domestic power and, in a mere few years, break relations with the Soviet Union and take Egypt squarely into the American camp. This process ultimately led to a rapid and unregulated neo-liberalization of the economy (the 'Open Door' policy), and to the deeply unpopular 1978 Camp David Accords with Israel, which led to the 1979 Egypt–Israel Peace Treaty.

The Bread Intifada of January 1977[4] was a major turning point in the regime's broader assault on the social compact of the Nasser years. Sadat deployed the army to crush the largely spontaneous mass protests that erupted in the wake of the regime's removal of basic food subsidies in line with IMF and World Bank demands. Scores died and hundreds were injured in the clashes, and the regime hastily conducted mass arrests of protestors and activists, writers and intellectuals across the broad spectrum of the left. Though Salih never explicitly discusses the Bread Intifada in the book, its ghost looms large in her analysis of the communist movement's historic inability to meaningfully

4 Dubbed 'riots' in the Western press and referred to as the 'Intifada of Thieves' in the state-controlled Egyptian press.

connect with labour and grassroots movements in Egypt.

Egypt's thriving communist movement reached its apogee in the 1940s at a time when the colonial political system with its fractious power-sharing arrangements between the British, the Egyptian monarchy and the liberal parties was at a breaking point. The post–Second World War order was characterized by mass protests that brought together a broad alliance of trade unions, left-wing nationalist groups, student and peasant organizations and the communist parties against the British and the Palace. The 1952 revolution, with its developing populist and anti-imperialist positions posed a new kind of problem for the communists in particular. On the one hand, here was a self-anointed revolutionary regime that seemed to be taking the country down the path of radical social and economic reform and offering demonstrable victories against Western imperialism. On the other hand, the regime's syncretic and statist vision of Arab socialism and its class structure were inimical to the most fundamental Marxist understanding of class struggle and revolutionary mass mobilization.

The new regime, however, understood only too well the threat to its existence posed by the communist movement. One of its first actions upon taking power was to violently repress a textile workers' strike in the industrial town of Kafr al-Dawwar. Two strike leaders were summarily executed and the rest of the leadership arrested and replaced by regime supporters. The years between 1959 and 1964 witnessed the round-up and incarceration of hundreds of communists. And yet many of these same communists emerged from their prisons to join hands with the regime that had fiercely attacked them. In 1965, the two main communist parties (Democratic Movement for National Liberation or HADITU; and the Egyptian Communist Party or ECP) voluntarily agreed to dissolve themselves and join Nasser's Arab Socialist Union. The regime absorbed these intellectuals and former militants as 'independent Marxists' working for the greater good of the revolution and of Arab socialism (and not incidentally, preserving good relations with the Soviet Union), and they in turn accommodated themselves to a reformist position within the regime's political and cultural institutions and propaganda organs. They became a neutered Marxist intelligentsia that gave the regime the requisite stamp of leftist legitimacy without ever securing a stable and effectively independent political or ideological base. Meanwhile, those who had refused the decision to dissolve were left homeless —locked out of state jobs and publication, harassed, detained, imprisoned and, in many cases, driven into exile.

This is the melancholy generation of the sixties that Salih returns to again and again in *The Stillborn*— those communist intellectuals and militants who were content 'to sing half a song' in Nasser's prisons and whose petty-bourgeois origins destined them to failure and defeat. This 'official' Nasserist left was inherited by Sadat in 1970. In spite of the first purges of his 1971 'corrective revolution', its leading lights continued to play their role as an institutional leftist flank until the regime itself brought an end to this historic accommodation as part of its move away from the Soviet camp into the US one. The public break and the wave of arrests that began in 1975 after the Sinai Interim Agreement with Israel, and that took on epic proportions in 1977 in the wake of the Bread Intifada effectively destroyed the public political base that the 'old guard' Nasserist wing of the sixties left had paid so dear to establish inside the regime. They had become a casualty of history.

The seventies student movement also ended in a historic defeat, but for different reasons. This is what forms the bulk of Salih's analysis in the book. The 'third-wave' left[5] that emerged from the movement was independent, and much more ideologically and tactically radical than its immediate predecessor. The ECWP was the biggest, most militant and most influential of the Marxist groups that emerged around the 1972–73 student movement. Though Sadat's declared 'victory' in the October War took the steam out of the

---

5 The term is Gervasio's, the first wave being the pre-1952 movement and the second wave that of the 1960s.

nationalist wing of the broader movement, the Marxist groups continued to agitate on and off campus (and to a lesser extent in labour-union circles) throughout the rest of the decade. Sadat's increasingly determined war on the left from 1975 on turned them into underground parties with various levels of secret organizational structure. This was the beginning of the vanguardism and structural 'alienation' that Salih so bitterly evokes in *The Stillborn*, and that she blames to a large extent for the tragic unravelling of the movement. The increasing state-sponsored Islamization of social and political life towards the end of the decade, and the 1979 peace treaty, were also nails in the coffin of the third-wave communist movement in Egypt.

The tragedy of the (post)colonial communist militant doomed to repetition by the national liberation struggle is one of the major themes of *The Stillborn*. As Salih notes in the updated introduction, 'the national struggle that haunts every sentence of the book' was a historical necessity for liberation-era communists. Palestine was a central site of this struggle, but there were others too: Algeria, Vietnam, Bolivia. The book's first chapter details the ways in which both second- and third-wave communists in Egypt were hopelessly trapped in the logic of anti-imperial nationalist populism, isolated from 'the only game in town' and forced to lead 'a double life' that destroyed both their integrity and 'their ability to believe'. The historic contradictions of this double position was a tragic legacy to the seventies student left. It had destroyed the communists of the previous generation, and it would also prove to be their own undoing after 1973.

This tragic history outlined in the book is paired, however, with farce: the spectacle of the upward trajectory of the socially mobile petty-bourgeois intellectual whose opportunism leads him to assume all kinds of untenable, even mercenary positions (Salih uses the terms 'intellectual', 'militant' and 'Marxist' interchangeably in the book). This is where the book does some of its most interesting work. Salih performs a kind of surgical operation on the figure of the (male) militant/intellectual across the two generations. The first chapter, 'The Intellectual as Pessimist', opens with an acerbic description of the 'nihilism' of the disillusioned militant emerged from his cell into the light of day—an attitude that she is at pains to distinguish from any kind of principled political philosophy, historical or otherwise, and that she defines as a kind of jumbled moral 'bag of tricks' that the 'liberated' and upwardly mobile former militant uses to justify his opportunism. This 'nihilism', and the resulting treason of the (sixties) intellectuals, is yet another bitter legacy to her own generation.[6] In the chapter, she

6 Salih uses an interesting mixed metaphor of Cold War maps and players to describe second-wave communists' positions towards the Nasser regime, which in some sense reflects her

discusses the momentous historical moment in which the student movement emerged (1967–73), and the multilayered story of political opportunism in the complex negotiations of the years following the October War, that brought an end to the movement, to revolutionary politics and to the national struggle all at once.

In Chapter Two, 'The Afterlives of the Student-Movement Generation', Salih builds on her description of this legacy as a vicious farce in which the unemployed and bitterly disillusioned 'fathers' of the sixties generation preyed upon their 'children' and instructed them in domination and venality. This point bears some explaining. The third-wave communism that emerged from the student movement was tutored by the independent sixties-era Marxists. These are the 'unemployed leaders' that Salih refers to at the opening of the chapter—those communists who had refused the voluntary party dissolutions of 1965 and who as a result were, at best, shut out of state employment and, at worst, sentenced to varying prison terms over the next few years. By the turn of the decade, some of the most brilliant among them had returned to public life and begun to form shifting and secret groups into which they recruited many of the young men and women organizers of 1972–73. The group

understanding of history as grand theatre (an understanding she revisits and revises as a form of kitsch in the book's updated introduction).

that eventually became the ECWP was notable for making a total break with the 'official' Nasserist left and undertaking a radical analysis of the bourgeois-technocratic bases of the regime. At the same time, the Stalinist structure of the various groups, their hyper-secrecy and their tendency to score-settling and sectarianism blocked the emergence of a real democratic left consciousness among the students. In Salih's estimation, this was the 'poisoned milk' that destroyed her generation of Marxists and ushered it into a new and ruinous postcolonial world order.

In the chapter, Salih offers a blistering critique of the Stalinism and sectarianism passed on to the student leaders of third-wave communism by their sixties generation mentors and discusses the destructive legacy of the vanguardism that was partly imbibed from the same source, and partly a product of the political conditions of the times which forced any kind of revolutionary organizing underground. She blames this vanguardism for the movement's total alienation from the everyday world of politics and the realities faced by 'ordinary people'. But the petty-bourgeois class origins of the intellectuals were also to blame for this state of affairs. Her analysis of the complex class structure of the postcolonial Egyptian intelligentsia is indeed central to her broader critique of the communist movement and its historic failure. Both generations were victims of their genetic appetite for social mobility.

Nasser's 'new class' of technocrats and functionaries rose from the diverse ranks of the Egyptian petty bourgeoisie to become a propertied bourgeois aristocracy of sorts, thanks to the lucrative nationalizations and state contracts of the 1960s. Their rebellious 'children', meanwhile, were able to comfortably fall back into this class base when the student movement fell apart. Others managed to parlay their militant past into new forms of social capital: foreign university degrees, jobs in international NGOs, gainful employment in the new and lucrative Gulf media industry. The rest either languished in some forgotten corner of irrelevance and despair, became buffoons at the tables of the new elite or managed to make quick money in the rushed and chaotic pillage of the national economy that was Sadat's Open Door. What all of these militant afterlives shared was the 'nihilism' that becomes, in Salih's reading, the general condition of Egyptian society by the end of the decade.

Salih's exploration of property and possession as the fundamental lynchpins of successful upward mobility in postcolonial Egypt includes a biting analysis of love, marriage and the family. She discusses the social and sexual mores of the bourgeois couple and the class structure of the family as one important element of the (petty) bourgeois intellectual's social pathology. It is this social pathology that is the subject of Chapter Three—'The Intellectual in Love'—the

shortest, most aphoristic and perhaps the most furi-
ous of the book's three chapters, with property (the
will to possess) and the symbolic violence of sexual
relations being the twin poles of analysis of the bourgeois male's brutal and brutalizing attitude to love.
The ghosts of Salih's own experience as a woman militant are most visible in this section of the book. It is
also the chapter where her subsequent exploration of
kitsch as a metaphor for this experience is already dis-
cernible, for example, in her description of the sexual
rituals of sadomasochistic repetition and the huckster
roles of mastery and possession that the intellectual
is obliged to enact as an escape from his spiritual
emptiness.

And yet Salih does not speak here from an explicitly feminist position or in the language of sexual liberation of second-wave feminism. Her position in this
regard is in many ways an ambivalent one. As mentioned earlier, the explicit object of much of the book's
critique is the masculine subject, and the critical perspective she offers is shot through and through with a
radically gendered experience. But Salih never fully
addresses the structural implications of this perspective, except in this last, short chapter, and here too in
a very specific way. The thorny question of feminism's
relationship to third-world liberation-era Marxism is
clearly visible here. Salih's translation of Tony Cliff's
Trotskyist work on women's liberation (see earlier) is

indicative of the way in which her generation of leftists considered feminism to be an adjunct to class struggle and not a distinct form of politics (an attitude still strong on today's Egyptian left). Her choice of the Arabic title for the book is even more telling: *On the Critique of the Feminist Movement*. As she points out in *The Stillborn*, the left feminism of the sixties and seventies in Egypt (in both its state and non-state forms) was a staid affair, one that was deeply implicated in the existing petty-bourgeois family structure and its engines of respectable social mobility. There was never a fully independent feminist movement, let alone a sexual revolution, in Egypt for a variety of structural reasons, a fact that may go some way in shedding light for the international reader on the language of sexual vice that is so central to Salih's analysis of the pathology of love in Egyptian bourgeois society, including, more to the point, in left and progressive intellectual circles.

The updated introduction and, particularly, the two letters appended to the end of the volume mark a dramatic shift into a personal mode. In the former, Salih attempts an answer to the question of why she became a communist. The move is both a form of private retrospection, or 'rendering of accounts', and a launching point for the book's interrogation of her former comrades—the much broader question of how 'to assess the truth of who we used to be'. To accomplish this, she turns to the notion of kitsch deployed by Milan Kundera in his novel *The Unbearable Lightness of Being*. Revolutionary kitsch, Salih tells us, is the key to untangling the disastrous imbrication of 'private motivation' and 'the call to duty' that shapes the militant psyche. 'The dangerous leap of faith' into thin air that the militant undertakes in order to realize the categorical agreement of being which is the 'dream' of revolution lands her in the deadening space of ideology; a space that refuses 'the human being as a world unto herself, alive with contradiction'. The result of this landing is an alienation so complete that madness or cynicism (i.e. 'nihilism') is the only possible outcome.

The letters—the first written in Cairo in 1988, the second written from her self-imposed exile in Spain in 1985—take this line of questioning even further. In these private letters, Salih constantly uses the tropes of loss, lack and impotence to reflect on her inability to *live* the utopian modes-of-being of a properly Marxist project. Again and again, she attempts to reach into the substratum of ideology in order to touch its emancipatory essence: a form of deep ethical knowledge and praxis beyond theory and party lines. The letters are full of the vocabulary of crushed dreams, lost illusions and shattered selves. As such, they serve as an important background to the stringent analysis and the terse, captious tone of the rest of the book.

In her posthumously published fragment of memoir, Salih tells the story of the destruction of her 'lost book'; the diaries that she had written both before and during her time as a member of the ECWP. Upon quitting the party, her comrade and lover of the time had got her to hand over the papers on party orders, supposedly against her possible arrest. Twenty years later, she discovered that he had lied to her; that it was he, and not the party, who desired to 'spare her the humiliation' of discovery.

In the following passage, she returns to her time in Spain; a halcyon period when her lifelong struggle with alienation and loneliness found an outlet of sorts in the freedom of physical estrangement:

> I used to walk for hours, and talk to myself the whole time. The world I observed around me was so much more human than what I'd been used to back home. Gardens and public love . . . long walks down light-hearted streets where teenagers exchange kisses without fear.

It was a solitude that gave her the permission to acknowledge her profound bitterness against the party, and against 'the intellectual as a species, in all its varieties'. Walking became her last refuge upon her reluctant return to 'the ugliness of life' in Cairo, a hallucinatory state of waking dream that cut her off once and for all from the world around her. In one of the most moving passages in the fragment, she describes

how, on one of these walks, she stopped on Sixth
October Bridge in downtown Cairo to gaze at the water
below, when two young men pass by and laugh at her:

'Are you going to do it, or what?'

I waited till they'd moved on, and jumped.

Generation and inheritance are useful tropes for
thinking about the global decline of the left in the
second half of the twentieth century. The 1970s
launched the neoliberal era that swept across the
planet and seemingly culminated in 'the end of history' in 1989. Except that it turned out history had not
ended after all, and the second decade of the twenty-
first century witnessed mass uprisings against the new
world order of the global bourgeoisie. Everyone who
lived and fought, laughed and cried on Egypt's streets
in 2011 tasted 'the sweetness of the moment of pure
freedom, of unbearable lightness', of which Salih
writes 20 years earlier. The uprising of 2011 was just
such a leap of faith, and one whose painful and furtive
afterlives are only just beginning to unfold. In the original introduction, Salih declares that she wrote her
book precisely as a warning to the future: 'to draw for
future generations the portrait of an inheritance that
they must repudiate'.

The legacies of compromise, cynicism and violated innocence that played out in and after the student uprising of 1972–73 ultimately took the form of

kitsch. The general devastation into which Salih's generation emerged from their closeted, self-consuming
circles led them to pose as victims weeping over the
ruins instead of honestly facing the role they had
played in the catastrophic outcome of the revolution.
They grimly fell back into picking up their pieces in
confusion and private shame, and turned to nostalgia
(the present as 'historic error') and personal rituals of
empowerment in order to exorcize a failure that must,
above all, not be named. But legacies are ambivalent
things. The hundreds of thousands of young men and
women who took the streets in 2011 were also haunted
by the ghosts of the past; their language, their songs
and symbols, their remembering of bygone battles all
drew on a history rich with the struggle for freedom.
And yet that moment of unbearable lightness was also
followed by utter ruin on a new and perhaps unprecedented scale. And so the same questions will surely
return to haunt this generation as it did the ones
before: Who were we? What was our experience? How
do we assess the truth of who we used to be?

Samah Selim
New York, November 2016

An Unavoidable Preface on Militant Kitsch

I wrote the material collected in this little book about five years ago but, due to circumstances beyond my control, the original publication was delayed until the present moment. When I reread the first chapter once I'd finally received the proofs, I was startled into a revelation. The book was divided into two main parts. The first part covered the political conditions that underpinned the eruption and decline of the student movement in the 1970s. The second part took up, first, that generation's relationship to the generation before it— the left intellectuals of the 1960s—and second, the fate of this student movement after its collapse. The rest of the book can be characterized as secondary impressions or addendums to these two main parts. Rereading the first chapter on politics disturbed me deeply because I realized that I now felt profoundly disconnected from the 'national struggle' that haunts every sentence of the book. It was obvious that my mind had been working overtime trying to answer some vital questions. One of these, in a somewhat different form, was: What happened to the national liberation project?

When I wrote the book I told myself that it was for 'the next generation' and, as luck would have it, I came face to face with my desired audience. This was a group of intellectuals and poets who belonged to what, for simplicity's sake, we might call the eighties and nineties generations as a way of positioning them in relation to my own, which is known of course as 'the generation of the seventies' (and by 'generation' I mean those who reached political consciousness in this or that decade, being mostly in their twenties at its opening). I went to them with the manuscript of my little book, proud and full of hope as the saying goes. The comments were not slow in coming: 'Is this some kind of exercise in self-flagellation?' 'Why don't you write a novel instead?' 'Your book is a good document for historians, but it's not history' (which is actually true). But nobody bothered to address the ideas in the book, and if they did venture in that direction, no one, not even once, brought up the conundrum of the national liberation struggle that I had tired myself out trying to unlock. The one bit that everybody wanted to talk about wasn't even originally part of the book. These were the private letters that a seasoned writer friend persuaded me to include as personal 'documents'.

The shock of my meeting with 'the next generation' made me slowly come to understand that my political consciousness belonged, much more than I had realized, to the very past that I had set out to critique—condemn even. It was an understanding of the world that viewed the present as a kind of 'historic error', as one of my interlocutors put it, or as *geist* (the phenomenology of spirit that came to our generation from Hegel via Marx). For in spite of all the bitterness that my generation (who were all leftists in one way or another) feels towards Gamal Abdel Nasser's regime and his era, they are fast prisoners of their nostalgia for that time. Herein lay the most glaring paradox of the book. This same period had witnessed the beginning of the student movement we had made, of its noisy birth as a generation. It was the first ever generation of the left that all of Egypt applauded; 'the generation that was rewarded for its nationalism before it had paid the price for it', as an old Marxist who had witnessed Nasser's purge of the communists in 1959 bitterly observed to me.[1] Even more importantly, this same generation was never able to imagine itself escaping the borders of the established political map that it eventually came to see as a pipe-dream: to the east the socialist camp, to the west the capitalist one and in the middle, at the very beating heart, the national independence movements of the third world. Our principles were Marxist–Leninist (or, more correctly, Hegelian, with all their metaphysics). We believed that we were a generation in full possession of the future. We believed that we were the repudiation of the Nasser era—its very antithesis, in fact, and

---

1 The mass arrests of communist militants, many of whom served five-year sentences in the Western Desert internment camps.

therefore its overcomer—and that we were the true representatives of the working class that would exile the Nasserist bourgeoisie from its expected paradise (this was the historical necessity—and, by the same token, the national one, of course). But in reality, we were nothing but bonded habitants of the Cold War map. We stood at its margins though—a communist opposition that built its one moment of glory on a transitional regime's inability to resolve the national question,[2] a tiny Marxist faction on a political map whose broader leadership and goals were nationalist.

In spite of all our Marxist nattering then, the language through which we chose to read our world (or which history chose for us) was nationalist, as was our historical consciousness. There is nothing to be ashamed of here. Rather, it was entirely logical. But the illusion of 'Marxist overcoming' in which we dealt (in our capacity as living specimens of the future planted in an ephemeral present) gave us an equivocal consciousness that led us into extremely complicated positions on both the intellectual and personal levels. When the map dissolved around us—spontaneously, and not through 'overcoming' or socialist revolutionary action—and when the Nasser era had faded into a

---

2 [The Anwar Sadat regime accomplished the transition from the anti-colonial nationalist populism of the Nasser era to the comprador neoliberalism of the Hosni Mubarak regime. (All footnotes that appear within square brackets have been added by the translator for this English-language edition.)]

hazy, indistinct past, we discovered that we had lost our way and that there was nothing to clutch at in the darkness but nostalgia. We were stripped down to our nakedness as we confronted a present that in no way conformed to our revolutionary prophecies. So we began to wail and cry over these dark times as compared, of course, to Nasser's era; he who now seemed to rise like an ancient idol, smiling at us, half-pitying and half-mocking across the decades. Our heroic deeds were the bequest of his era, and their domain had faded away with it. We still weep over the tiny role we played on his vast map, and over the beautiful dream that we would one day make it anew (side by side with our exalted comrades in the Soviet Union). We searched the miscreant present for a crevice to release the ghosts of the past—ghosts of the nation, of course, not of the working classes. The new map moved the masses of the Egyptian people back into the fold of religion while our generation continued to cling to its old faith. After the breakup of the Soviet Union, comrades meeting by chance would greet each other with the question: 'Are you still a believer?'

That old and very small part we played was, at least, a role. When it faded away, our generation held on to its icons like relics, muttering incantations of self-preservation until that day when times changed and the land of milk and honey would finally be made real. But our new role on this remade map lacked the beauty of the innocent old illusion. In the new, pious Egypt, we became the vanguard of the pious.[3] It was as though we found ourselves standing in the same marginal spot, on the same map, only in reverse, like a ghostly negative image.

In one of the private letters published in this book, I ask myself why I became a communist. I then apologize and write that a militant should never have to ask herself this question in the first place. To anyone who picks up this book without reading this new preface, the question will seem to contradict the nationalist certitudes in the first part. But reading backwards, I can see the traces of how my thinking was already changing. For example, I no longer believe that the Israeli state is more vicious or oppressive than its neighbours (and may my former comrades forgive me if they can). It is simply the stronger state. Moreover, I confess, with grief, to now believing that a future Palestinian state— if it ever comes into being—will almost certainly also be built on inequality and exploitation.[4] Is this a kind

3 [Salih's play on 'piety' here refers both to the steady Islamization of Egyptian society in the 1970s, which was partly driven by the regime's strategy of crushing the Left (Sadat referred to himself as 'the pious president') and to the vanguardism of the new communist parties after 1975.]

4 [This preface was written in 1996, three years after the Oslo Accords brought the first Palestinian intifada to an end and set the stage for the undoing of the PLO and accelerating Israeli occupation of Palestinian lands.]

of post-nationalist 'nihilism'? At the present moment, absolutely.[5] There is nothing inspiring about the massacres taking place in the name of nationalism all over the world today. They are abhorrent to me, as are racism and religious fanaticism. Even our precious class consciousness has been guilty in this respect. Is this then an outright condemnation of our past struggle? Judging after the fact is always difficult. Perhaps all one can say is that we engaged our own history passionately and in a way that made sense at the time. Apart from that, I can only say that the desire to conjure the past into the present is a profoundly ahistorical impulse. History's judgement is clear, however. It abandoned the proprietors of truth and, knowing my comrades well, this was for the best. The history that mocked not only our humble student movement but the victories of the French Revolution itself, along with the entire tradition of radical human thought of the eighteenth and nineteenth centuries, is not a *quiddity* —not some spirit that floats in the ether and passes judgement, applauding militants who move the wheel forwards and threatening those who impede its progress. History is constructed by human beings who

---

5 Of course, no one has the right to expect the Palestinians to cease struggling for their rights and common interests, but slapping qualifiers like 'truth' on history and those who make it is what I now find to be entirely idealistic, and 'nationalistic'—a word that has now clearly come to mean 'specious'.

are not 'made of different clay', as the communists once described Stalin, and its course is most often determined by the worst of them. One final confession remains, and perhaps some may find satisfaction in it: I know very well that my current positions are those of an intellectual on the margins who merely observes events and cannot affect their outcomes. This is not political preaching, but simply a personal shift in my reading of history that I recount as it is.

And what about us then? What is left to us? What do we do with the burden of this past? We offer the new generations our pious martyrdom with a tender, teary-eyed smile, and they observe us as though we were mummies preserved in the museum of history—mummies that they regard with the neutrality of the truly wretched. How do we assess the truth of who we used to be? Perhaps this was the most honest—but also oblique—question that the book asked. And so now, allow me to bring up the subject of revolutionary kitsch.

In one of his books, Muhammad Hasanayn Haykal[6] (for whom I have a deep political aversion)

---

6 [Muhammad Hasanayn Haykal (1923–2016): Notorious and prolific Egyptian journalist and author. He was a political cadre of both the Nasser and Sadat regimes in his capacity as member of the Central Committee of the Arab Socialist Union. He served as editor-in-chief of the government-owned Egyptian daily *Al-Ahram* for 17 years (1957–74) and continued to be a major commentator on Arab and Egyptian affairs till his death.]

discusses the psychological make-up of the young men who join militant organizations, both communist and Islamist. Haykal claims that these are all individuals who seek the warmth and protection of the group (and I apologize for not remembering the title of the book or the exact passage). The young man who joins a militant (or jihadist) group is then, for him, a problem. At least this, in a nutshell, is the portrait offered by a writer who is, first, a political opponent and, second, a man who himself came of age under the state's warm wing (and who is therefore not 'a problem'). Why did we join the militant organizations that proliferated in our day? Were we answering the call of history? This is what any one of us would have unhesitatingly responded if asked back in those days. Or was the reason more obscure and personal than that, as Haykal suggests? The young member of a religious organization today responds to 'God's call', and I can well understand why he feels indignant when media analysts dissect his liberation project into bits and pieces of personal despair and sexual repression. But there is a little bit of truth in Haykal's method. The militant is someone who responds to a form of collective awareness. He steps into the movement for the sake of correcting the ever-crooked balance of truth and history. At the same time, each tries—with honour, if possible—to grapple with their personal demons (and there is nothing shameful in this as the talented Mr Haykal surely knows). No one has the

right to hold a militant (or *mujahid*) accountable for
his private motivations or to drag his demons into the
light, except as a form of literature or testimony. In any
other form, this kind of 'outing' is a politically despicable act.

Between private motivations and 'the public call',
however, there is an in-between ground that the great
Czech writer Milan Kundera called 'kitsch'.[7] Kitsch,
according to Kundera, is a nineteenth-century German
Romantic word meaning 'trash' and has come to refer
to the 'vulgar' art and literature deployed by postmod-
ernism. Kundera uses the word in a specific sense,
however—as a type of violent sentimentalism embod-
ied in the collective dream of salvation. According to
Kundera, all ideologies have their own forms of kitsch:
Catholic, Protestant, Jewish kitsch; communist, fascist, democratic, feminist kitsch; nationalist and inter-
nationalist, and now, of course, Islamist kitsch. For
leftists, there is the Great March—that illustrious
international journey towards brotherhood, equality,
justice and happiness (isn't it wonderful to dream of
being one of multitudes marching forwards across the
ages?). 'What makes a leftist a leftist is not this or that
theory but his ability to integrate any theory into the

---

7 From *The Unbearable Lightness of Being*. The novel is about
the relationship between men and women (their lightness and
heaviness), freedom and responsibility. All the quotations that
follow are taken from the novel. And no one should be tempted
to shoot the novelist.

kitsch called the Grand March. [. . .] In the realm of totalitarian kitsch, all answers are given in advance and preclude any questions.' For this reason, kitsch is the ideal of all politicians and political movements: 'It follows then that the true opponent of totalitarian kitsch is the person who asks questions.'[8] The specificity of Kundera's definition of kitsch falls exactly at the meeting point between 'the public call' (or the call to duty) and private motivation. This is what he calls 'the categorical agreement of being'[9]—the burning desire of those who live in discord with themselves and the world projected into an abstraction of human lack and incompleteness (the unbearable lightness of being). They desperately seek wholeness—a weight to root them in the world, or a sense of continuity in the face of death. They are obsessed with the crack in human existence that hovers between dream and reality, hope and impossibility and produces great genius as well as despair, failure and many varieties of crime.

'The categorical agreement of being' carries a fundamental contradiction. In order for it to be generative, it requires a dangerous leap of faith, summoned at a moment's notice: the euphoria of transcending the necessity of being. We have all known—even the

8 [Milan Kundera, *The Unbearable Lightness of Being* (Michael Henry Heim trans.) (London: Faber & Faber, 1984), pp. 257, 254.]

9 [Ibid., p. 248.]

worst among us—the sweetness of this moment: a moment of pure freedom, of unbearable lightness. And this is where the danger lies. Enter the mythical circle of collective salvation—worship its kitsch and madness beckons. You will not allow a word spoken against your piety; you refuse the human being as a world unto herself, alive with contradiction. People become objects to be carefully laid on Procrustes' bed. You chop off this one's head and stretch that one's leg, to make him fit on the bed. You become heavier than the stone lid of a coffin carved of certitude.

'Kitsch excludes everything from its purview which is essentially unacceptable in human existence.'[10] Kundera describes this structure of kitsch as communist society itself, the Party being 'liberated territory' in bourgeois society (our comrades used to say the same thing). It is a certitude that comfortably and confidently refuses all difference, and demands stupid submission to its chosen idols: 'the smiling brotherhood' in the Great March, or on God's path, it matters little. The most shocking of communism's massacres and countless petty treasons have been the fruit of this certitude, and this was so even in our organizations which never had the chance to hold power. Today, the same faith inspires pious young men with the cold-blooded hearts of murderers. 'As soon as kitsch is recognized for the lie it is, it moves into the context of

10 [Ibid.]

non-kitsch, thus losing its authoritarian power and becoming as touching as any other human weakness.'"[11] But you cannot recognize the lie unless, worn out with exhaustion, you make the return journey from that place of radiant faith with brute honesty as your only companion. To what do you return then? To bourgeois society (the prodigal son)? To the self? To an old and always elusive dream? The possibilities are endless and it's all up to you in the end.

At the beginning of this preface, I posed the question of who we truly were. I think that everyone must simply shoulder his own burden in this. Our collective truth is that our history and class (petty bourgeois for most of us) will remain as only one part of the story for anyone who managed to preserve some shreds of his or her individuality in the face of the onslaught of kitsch (though I doubt this is possible, for even those who cling to communist kitsch today do so precisely because they are incapable of realizing their individuality outside of it). In this book, I've tried to sketch this first part of the truth. Who were we? What was our experience? In other words: How did we come to be defeated? And finally, in the second part of the book: What did we do with that defeat? I don't think that if I were to write this book now, I would change much in spite of my explicit disagreement with what I wrote back then. I've left the first (political) part more or less

11 [Ibid., p. 256.]

as is—as a living portrait of a distant past; an example of the way an entire generation thought about the national struggle and a mirror of its contradictory consciousness, simultaneously Marxist and nationalist—because it all remains 'true' in terms of the work as a whole.

The last and most difficult question ('Why did I become a communist?') is left to the private letters published here. I've already mentioned the shock I had upon rereading the political part of the book. It raised the whole question of why I had been interested in politics in the first place (the bogeyman of private motivations: I think I can now understand the feelings of the ex-Islamist towards the theological disputes of his former brothers. Kitsch has fallen away and he stands face to face with his hidden motivations). It's strange to suddenly realize that the journey you spent your entire life making began with no real love for its actual, declared, shared object (political militancy) but, rather, with the unbearable weight of 'the call to duty'—though the letters perhaps say otherwise. Other meanings lie behind the words politics and history, nation and class, struggle and the people, other keys to their power that send us back to adolescence. The book is deeply preoccupied with ethics: ethics as the incomplete and impotent individual self's means of regulating the chaos of life, a self that gleans the world's injustice—that which must not be—and goes forth on a passionate quest for justice and that which must be, with the special sensitivity of the wounded . . . Such treasure! For this self, denuded of kitsch and standing alone, the militant's journey becomes a quest for ethical knowledge, an overcoming that is constantly creative and penetrating. This is the knowledge I tried to seek here between the lines, behind the talk of class and politics, and behind the portraits of individuals presented as abstractions; knowledge snatched with a kind of ferocity from the certitudes of the past, a type of justice that I have learnt to discover to the extent that I have pursued it. For this reason, I offer the reader this book—which here settles into its final form—as something like a crossword puzzle whose solution lies here in this preface.

Introduction

This work examines the experience of the student-movement generation—the generation that was in its early twenties in 1972 and 1973, when thousands of university students took to the streets in every Egyptian city and raised a demand which might sound strange today: war with Israel. The demonstrations were met with massive popular support and ordinary people were suddenly moved from the state of despair brought about by the June Defeat[1] to the heights of joy. It was as though the demonstrations were a magic sword suddenly raised to challenge the fast chains of the defeat that had been pronounced by 'nationalist' intellectuals to be our collective destiny. The demonstrations carried an obscure promise of deliverance, a promise that sank into oblivion under the rubble of a twisted history with no room for inflated dreams.

The book is a return then, to the time of defeat. But it is also a return—though it may seem a paradox—to a time when to speak of the dreams of the nation elicited serious and impassioned discussions in every home, rather than the contempt and ridicule

1 [The Six-Day Arab–Israeli War of 1967 in which Israel occupied the West Bank and Gaza, the Golan Heights and the Sinai Peninsula. The war is often referred to in the Arab world simply as 'The Defeat' (al-hazima).]

it does today. Before this period, life under Gamal
Abdel Nasser seemed to be more wonderful than any
dream. The poor were getting an education and the
door to social mobility was thrown wide open. Victories over imperialism succeeded one after the other,
jubilant news of the great leader's conquests were
broadcast into people's homes without them having
had to lift a finger. Anyone suspicious of this dream
was considered a madman or a mutant and condemned to be an outcast. But the June Defeat mercilessly ripped this dream apart and led to a flurry of
collective self-interrogation. We were a people trying
desperately to retrieve its ability to think after a long
age of inanity. The regime, whose crude prestige had
been broken by the Defeat, left us alone to play this
dangerous game for a while. Intellectuals and the
educated classes more broadly rushed to reopen all the
forbidden files. Artists and writers dared the censors,
their 'dangerous' works welcomed by a population
thirsty for inspiration, a population not yet destroyed
by apathy and despair. This was why the time after the
Defeat was on every level the most dynamic period of
the July-revolution regime's life[2]—a dynamism that
was absent before 1952 and even after the 'victory' of

---

2 ['The July-revolution regime' is a term that insists on the
continuity of the post-1952 state and military-political order in
spite of the transitions of power between ostensibly different
administrations.]

October 1973. It was during this time that the student movement began.

This short book does not, however, revisit the period and its various actors as a whole. Instead, it focuses on the student groups that vigorously channelled the energy of the street to organize and lead the protests in the name of an insurgent dream: to change the future of the nation, to save it. The naivety of this striving now provokes a smile—from my own generation more than any other. But what's much crueller, I think, is that the generations that came after ours never had the chance to know such vast ambition. This is why I've chosen to write about *our* aborted ambition. Because it was not just a mirage (as many of us today like to describe it in order to mortify the past, a kind of reaction against our youthful arrogance, I suppose). It was also a history with real effects, and I find it strange that we should squander our insights into this history just because we ourselves were defeated with humiliating ease. The memories I have preserved of this time bear witness to the vital life-worlds of our people and our intellectuals, and this in spite of the pain of remembering. I do believe in the end that history is not quite so dark.

I write here of that generation, of the outbreak and abrupt end of the student movement, of the experience of its 'young leaders', the sources of their inspiration and their special relationship to the generation that preceded them, the left intellectuals of the 1960s. It was in many ways a unique historical context: the euphoric rise of Nasser's era and then its raging collapse—a collapse that succeeded against all odds in seizing the entire nation by the throat and finishing off the historical situation in which the student movement was born and briefly thrived. Then we found ourselves in an entirely new situation with different cares and dreams; a situation which made the student movement, and that whole upstart generation of intellectuals and militants, superfluous.[3] Barely launched on its journey into politics, art and science, it was quashed along with the world it had attempted to bring into being. It grew suddenly old; its children became incomplete projects—a stillborn generation.

The subject of this little book, then, is not history and politics even when it delves into these subjects. Rather, the book traces the experience and trajectory of a generation with features quite different from those of its political and intellectual predecessors. Various sections of the book examine the context in which this generation took root, its vision and understanding of the political circumstances in which it moved, and the unfolding of personal destinies in the wake of its defeat. For this reason I find it necessary to clarify here

---

3 [The reference is to the onset of Sadat's 'Open Door' economic reforms and the regime's submission to the imperialist status quo in the region.]

that this work is neither a historical document nor a political polemic but, rather, a personal view of the events that created and shaped my generation.[4] In this sense alone, I assume full responsibility for the book. I intend it to be a truthful and consistent account, rather than a comprehensive or even objective one. On this note, I ought to mention that friends who read the text before it went to press reproached me for certain passages which they felt to be marked by a kind of ferocity or bitterness. It seems to me that those who are always keen to protect themselves from the hard knocks of experience are less capable of coming to terms with it. Their objectivity is a luxury that doesn't necessarily communicate a greater form of sincerity. It may be that the voice of the victim haunts the chapters that follow. Nonetheless, one of my major concerns in writing the book was to draw for future generations the portrait of an inheritance that they must repudiate, and in this I am not prepared to compromise.

Finally, I should like to apologize to the lovers and specialists of literature, some of whom among my acquaintances objected that the book belongs to no clear literary genre (some critics found it to be 'formally impoverished'). On this matter, I haven't much

---

4 Because of my dependence on this personal experience in writing the book, I exclude the events and leaders of the 1968 student strikes, whose situation was somewhat different from that of the seventies generation.

to say. I wrote the book with no prior decision about what form it should take. I was only concerned to transmit a particular experience and I did so in a manner that felt right to me, without the discipline of any literary rules—except for the most basic and necessary ones. All I can hope is that the message reaches the reader clearly: that I have succeeded in restoring to memory some of the contours of an era and of those who lived it. Except for this, I claim no particular literary value for this work. I do know that upon finishing the book and discovering that the story I tell here is the easiest part of truth, I deeply regretted my lack of literary talent.

CHAPTER ONE

The Intellectual as Pessimist

O heart of mine, please heed what I have to say,
You will need to have faith sometime, some day.
My heart shook and asked: What should I believe,
Believe in whom or what, tell me exactly, pray?

Salah Jahin[1]

1. *The Price of Rising to the Top*

The intellectual rejects the morality of all classes in the society that he denounces. But because the ethical human being is still a chimera, our intellectual discovers that there is nothing to take the place of the moral systems he repudiates. From his solid ground of bourgeois morality, he leaps up into the open air of freedom, only to find that he has gathered into himself the moral corruption of all classes. So he grows his beard and declares himself to be 'alienated'. Then, thanks to his native intelligence, he finally succeeds in securing a respectable position in society. From his comfortable armchair on the set of some television talk show (if he happens to make it that far), he might announce that

---

1 [Salah Jahin (1930–86): beloved Egyptian colloquial poet, playwright and cartoonist. Translated here and in subsequent references by Nehad Salem.]

he is a 'committed artist', and the audience is rightly bored to tears. So he shaves his beard and finally settles down to the conviction that vacuity is the sole truth of the world. His nihilism does not prevent him, however, from eating and drinking too much rich stuff at the elite gatherings to which he has gained admission thanks to his militant past. At the same time, he never forgets his old petty-bourgeois hatred for the class into which he has risen, and he also takes much pleasure in secretly despising anyone and everyone whose illusions remain intact. The feeling is mutual in any case: in these types of gatherings, a healthy sense of realism rules, and good food and drink are the only sure truth. Therefore, he is not lying when he claims that nihilism is his last religion.

2. *Waiting for a Post*

This is just one type of pessimist intellectual in our country today. There are many roads to nihilism these days, and there's now a permanent seat at the council of nihilism for the 'Marxist' looking for a new role to play. In the sixties, the intellectual's role was scripted by the Nasser regime: a reasonable prison sentence, discharge, then a job in one of the regime's bustling bureaucracies. The Marxist intellectual had one of two choices: he could either sing from behind the bars of his cage or wither away in a crushing tomb of solitude. The walls of this tomb were the *tableau vivant* of the people rallying around their great leader. He knew much more than he could fully speak and yet he was incapable of self-murder in his tomb of silence. And so he settled down to sing half a song and never forgave himself for it. He condemned himself even more mercilessly than those who condemned him. These were his first steps on the road to nihilism.

3. *The Untimely Downfall*

One of the ironies of this bitter life—or of history, if you prefer—is that our generation of seventies intellectuals or leftists or militants (and their imitators in many cases), which was so cruel in denouncing the revolutionaries of the preceding generation—their flabbiness and despair and even their perfidy—readily took its seat at the great feast of nihilism without having sung even half a song. We truly believed that making history was quite an easy thing—how young and unseeing we were! And still, we cast about for a role that turned out to be even more pathetic than the one played by the sixties generation. The intellectuals of the sixties moved us deeply with their half-songs after all; with fiction and poetry whose melancholy pierced through all the lies and made something that deserved to be called art, great art even. But history didn't spare them, and it rushed us along before we had even begun. We are the children of a time in which even 'melancholy lost its halo' and became something dreary and tedious, like a common cold, or a headache,[2] and tedium does not produce art, only tedious individuals.

4. *Two Stories from the Same Trench*

What the two generations shared, the most unquestionable continuity, and also the strangest and most tragic, was that remarkable combination of radical intellectual positions and nihilist sensibility. Incongruity is the basis of all truth it seems. Failure and defeat were at the very heart of this combination, if in different ways and for different reasons. Historical circumstance was stronger than the militants of the the sixties, who were swept away by Nasser's victories. And then, of course, the Soviet state secured the bourgeoisies of the third world while punishing dissidents in the socialist camp and keeping everyone else on a tight leash. The sixties generation were the offspring of Egypt's last popular mass movement; this was the experience that shaped them. And then they suddenly found themselves in a new and strange time, living under a regime that brutally suppressed 'the people' in whose name it claimed to rule. They were victims of a violent transition between two historical moments, both of which were difficult to defend. They became alienated, first from the masses, because they refused to believe in the regime that had enchanted everyone

---

2 May our great poet rest in peace. [Salah Jahin, *Quatrains*]

with its 'triumphs', then from themselves, because they were incapable of resisting a regime that claimed to be leading the battle against imperialism (a lonely and utterly heroic battle in the eyes of the watching masses). If the militant of the sixties had actually managed to oppose the regime thoroughly and completely, the only good it would have done would have been to isolate him totally from the only struggle in town, the only one of real interest to the masses. This is why part of him was always attached to the regime—a regime that constantly alternated between rallying and persecuting the people in the name of the nation. Boundaries that used to be clear enough—between truth and falsehood, enemy and ally, right and wrong—disintegrated. What was to be done and what was not to be done? There was no longer a reliable standard to go by, not even from a Marxist perspective. So the militant of the sixties was pulled here and there, alone and estranged from one and all. Inevitably, he led a double, even triple life. No wonder then that he lost the one thing that sustained the integrity of his being: the ability to believe.

As for us, we too were overcome by the bitter irony of history. The same regime whose victories against imperialism had knocked them off their feet for years ravaged us with its defeat in June 1967. The faithful masses were dragged along in the mud (for they had always stood behind their leader) and when they finally woke up, the damage had already been done.

We had imagined that we were the children of a new era, an era in which the people would finally declare their independence from the Nasser regime, but we were wrong. In reality, the student movement was a cornerstone of the regime's mythology, contrary to what some of its former leaders might think today.[3] The masses who took to the streets in the wake of the Defeat did not stand with us to the extent we like to imagine. They had not lost faith in the regime to the same degree. The leaders of the student movement arrived at their faith through very different channels — through their link to the dissidents of the previous generation, and to the progressive intellectual climate of the Nasser-era intelligentsia as a whole. Their revolt was not rooted in an independent tradition of popular mass struggle—the conditions for it didn't exist. The political climate was one in which Marxism and Marxists were 'tolerated' as harmless dreamers. The regime would nevertheless occasionally steal bits from the language of Marxism to make up for the poverty of the bourgeois thought which was its real—not borrowed—ideological basis. The language of the international bourgeoisie at the time of Nasser's rise to power was not fitted to people's dreams of changing the world. It was this same bourgeoisie that invented the 'pragmatism' that chokes us to death today. The

---

3 I hope those who object to being called 'leaders' in this context will exercise their patience as the designation won't be in circulation for much longer.

Nasserist vision got all tangled up with Marxism, and it became increasingly difficult to distinguish between the two until well after the flood waters had receded.

5. *The Student Movement: A Beginning or an Ending?*

The street was decidedly Nasserist in its perspective; there was no consciousness of what might differentiate it and hold it apart. There were perhaps occasional glimpses of a 'return to consciousness'[4] but nothing more. The impoverished masses had not yet severed their ties to the regime. The people wanted the regime to go to war. It never occurred to them that anybody else could wage the battle against colonialism (the regime had trained them to believe this). They themselves certainly couldn't do it—and all alone no less! Nor did it occur to the students whom we set out to persuade of the necessity of fighting a popular war of

---

4 [In 1972, shortly after Sadat's 'Corrective Revolution', the iconic and elderly 'liberal-era' Egyptian author and playwright, Tawfiq al-Hakim, published a controversial mea culpa in which he attacked Nasser and the 1952 Revolution. Though *The Return of Consciousness* ('Awdat al-wa'y) aligned al-Hakim with Sadat's political agenda, al-Hakim went on to pen the famous February 1972 writers' declaration demanding the release of the university students who had been imprisoned in the wake of the first burst of protests that year. In her phrasing, Salih uses the word *isti'ada* instead of *'awda* to denote 'return'. The difference is important. While *'awda* ascribes agency to consciousness itself (consciousness 'returns'), *isti'ada* denotes the human agent's active role in 'bringing back' or re-claiming consciousness.]

liberation, that we were asking them to part ways with the regime. Perhaps if we had remained suspended in that situation (which became famously known as the state of 'not-war and not-peace') for long, a truly independent popular movement might have really taken off. But the word 'perhaps' in relation to history throws open the door to the devil's mischief. Who would have had the patience to wait for that 'perhaps' to come to pass in a state of not-war and not-peace? Sadat certainly didn't wait. Instead, in these conditions, the student movement actually made him speed up the peace negotiations with Israel and aborted any possibility of a mass movement. The people had never known what it meant to be independent of the regime and its interests. How then could they have had an independent perspective on what was happening? They were fated to follow the road to its very end before waking up to the reality of their separateness, their independence. The regime meanwhile still had a long way to go in order to gradually come to terms with the concessions required of it under the hanging sword of the occupation.[5] It was a bloody road of war and death whose ultimate destination was surrender.

---

5 It is well known that the Sadat who went to Jerusalem is the same Sadat who had earlier rejected the Rogers initiative accepted by Nasser while on a trip abroad. [The Rogers Plan was a framework proposed by the US secretary of state William P. Rogers to achieve a a ceasefire in the Arab–Israeli conflict following the Six-Day War and the War of Attrition (1967–70).]

The student movement was the expression of this transitional moment in the life of the Nasser regime.[6] The masses only ever gained a measure of independent consciousness in step with the regime's developing positions. The explosion of the student movement onto the political scene was the result of a crack in the walls of the regime's house, a house of which it was still, nonetheless, the undisputed master. The masses were sympathetic to the student movement because it 'pressured' the regime, not because it sought to over- turn it. From the people's point of view, there was as yet no strong justification for outright antagonism.

It was no coincidence then, that the student move- ment was the hero of the day, and that the broader public looked on with an innocent delight out of step with the climate of struggle. The people were not con- scious of belonging to distinct classes with distinct interests in the conflict. They did not understand the principle of actively independent social relations. These relations were muddy and obscure; any approach to them was only possible through the iron gates erected by the leader and his official spokesmen. The masses were 'unified' around a national struggle that the regime alone defined; they were ignorant of the

6 [Salih's position here (and that of the ECWP) is that contrary to appearances and to the analysis of Nasserist intellectuals, the Sadat regime represented a continuation of the Nasser regime rather than a decisive break with it.]

class interests at stake. How then was it possible to suppose that a serious struggle could arise in such a situation when the opposing parties didn't even acknowledge the difference between them? When they weren't even aware of the existence of a domestic conflict? According to the regime, the danger was all ostensibly external, and whatever Nasser said had to be true. How could anyone have seen him as a domestic threat when he had destroyed 'exploitative capital' and 'the agents of colonialism'?

It was natural that the first protests would be as vague and equivocal as these murky class relations: neither the forces who opposed them nor those who supported them were clearly defined. Even the regime didn't object to the positions taken by the student movement, which were cryptic and ambiguous: peace *and* the demand to go to war in order to restore the country's wounded dignity (as yet inseparable from the dignity of the regime).[7] This was the heart of the matter. People had grown accustomed to the regime speaking on their behalf and on behalf of their interests. They could not see that behind its flabby nationalist jargon, behind its analysis of the national 'struggle' (whose ambitions were growing more minuscule by

---

7 I refer here to the actual masses of protesting students and not to what was in the heads of the leaders. It is worth mentioning that the regime's repression of the 1972–73 demonstrations was like a pat on the back compared to the repression of the mass protests of 1977.

the year) the regime was intent above all on preserving its own existence. Everything else was up for negotiation, including what mattered most to the masses, the interests of the nation. The nation, the regime and the people were supposedly all the same thing, without distinction. So when the regime managed to save its own skin and the national struggle fell to pieces, the people had not yet begun to understand the real measure of difference between the these two things. Because of this, the aftermath of the war was completely mystifying; no one understood that the regime had been fighting to save itself, not the country as a whole. The dust of the battles—or, rather, the courage of those who fought them—obscured the interests that had been served by the war. The regime meanwhile was saved from punishment by its colour blindness, a blindness imposed on us too by the 'white revolution' they so loved to trumpet.[8] This was basically the secret of the 'national unity' that spoilt the student movement and made it lose its head. It was especially true of its leaders, some of whom may well have been haunted by images of the revolution of 1919.[9] There is some truth to the historical comparison. Unchallenged

---

8 [The 1952 Revolution.]

9 [The Egyptian revolution of 1919 was a mass-based nationalist uprising against the British occupation and the latifundist bases of the monarchy. It led to the establishment of a constitutional parliamentary system in Egypt and the beginning of negotiations with the British for independence.]

national consensus is a clear sign that the bourgeoisie remains firmly in charge of the popular movement. This is the class that always claims to speak in the name of the people even when it is bent on betraying them.

The student movement, however, got what it had demanded. The regime waged an utterly useless war and silenced the movement for good in the process (that's really what happened!). When the regime went to war in 1973, it had given up on its illusions of 1967 about how to deal with the 'consequences of the aggression'. In 1967, the possibility of 'compromise solutions' with Israel and the United States was still on the table. Both these countries remained deeply suspicious of the regime—it had led them a merry dance in the past—so long as it retained even half a measure of national sovereignty or self-respect in its dealings with Israel (imperialism can also be described as 'extremist'). Formal recognition of Israel —meaning, recognition of Israel's right to the lands it had seized in 1948 and of its structure as a racist state—was not enough. Instead, the demand was for reconciliation and naturalization. In the same way, non-alignment was not enough: 'special' relations with the United States were required.[10] A reasonable share of our national economy was not enough; total

10 [US president Richard Nixon's visit to Egypt in 1974 formally initiated this process.]

liberalization was demanded, so that the economy could be pillaged more effectively in the rush to a 'free market' in which we ourselves would have no part. Nothing about this free market was free, of course. It was built on coercion and enforced hardship barely concealed by the thin veil of national sovereignty. At first, the regime calculated that the concessions would end with the first set of demands and convinced the people that this was in fact possible (easily, of course, because it had no competitors). But the real world was one of extremes: it had no room for Nasserist compromises. Times had changed. In 1967, it was no longer possible to repeat the same hand played in 1956.[11] The enemy now had been a patron back in the era of the ageing British lion, the strongman of the modern age—the United States itself. The regime learnt to be realistic during the Israeli occupation of Sinai. It discovered that the age of resistance and of all its grand projects to change the world was over. But it declined to inform the people of this. They were left in the dirt to pick over those sterile delusions for titbits with which to shame the bourgeois regime that had cheated them.

And so the dilemma that began in 1967 with the desire to minimize the concessions offered to the west

11 [A reference to the Suez War of 1956. Following Nasser's nationalization of the Suez Canal in July of that year, Britain, France and Israel invaded Egypt in October. The state of war officially ended in March of the following year thanks to US-led negotiations.]

and Israel—concessions that were no longer controversial in and of themselves—was transformed into
the dilemma of how the regime was to disembarrass
itself of the people's will, so that it could offer the same
concessions freely in 1973.

There is no doubt that Nasser was, as usual, quick
to smell which way the wind was blowing. This was
why he chose Sadat as his successor. He knew, of
course, that Sadat would be the one to provide the
solution,[12] that what was to come would require a president whose self-respect and scruples were highly elas-
tic, and that Sadat would not be outdone at grovelling.
The choice was eminently worthy of Nasser's wisdom
—but also of his cunning. Sadat's joy at becoming
'president' made him lose his mind to the extent that
he began to attack Nasser in public speeches long after
the man had actually died. But Sadat was not entirely
to blame for everything that happened, even though
Egypt never hated a ruler as much as it came to hate
him (not including the nouveau riche of the Open
Door era, of course). And even though Sadat's secret
files have not yet been fully laid open to historians, his
assassination bears witness to the fact that Nasser,

12 In *Autumn of Fury*, Haykal supports this interpretation when
he cites Nasser as having said that the West wanted to deal with
a president who would capitulate, and that he himself would not
be that man. Our great leader then personally chose the president who would capitulate so as not to leave anything to chance!
Haykal, however, insists that the matter was a coincidence.

dead, still had the last word. The two leaders' respective funerals speak for themselves.[13] The real victim of this grand prank however, was the people. Nasser made history from his grave as he made it while living. He turned himself into an idol raised high above the corpse of the masses who had worshipped him. In order for the idol's name to be sanctified, he manipulated an entire people so as to shift his ignominy onto someone else well after he himself had chosen the path the country would take. And so *we* were shamed and disgraced while *his* image continued to shine in glory. This was the last of Nasser's travesties—the only remaining trace of the era of 'national independence' and 'Arab socialism'.

In 1967, the regime's intention was to try to preserve what it could of its 'national achievements', and in 1973 came the realization that this was impossible. But for years now, the regime had been obliged to absorb and silence the people's anger with its 'preparations' for war. And so the inevitable came to pass. Sadat waged a limited war to please the people *and* offered unlimited concessions to the West, thereby saving his regime from the anger of both. Israel and

---

13 [Nasser's funeral in October 1970 was attended by 5 million mourners and the funeral cortege stretched for 10 kilometres. Sadat's funeral in 1981 was attended by three former US presidents and Menachem Begin, then prime minister of Israel. No Arab heads of state attended.]

the West were given everything they asked for gift-wrapped in our blood.[14]

In order for his strategy to be successful, Sadat represented the conflict with Israel in psychological terms. This is how a real war, made up of arms and money and human beings, became a device for absorbing the electrifying shocks of the successive concessions. Of course, he didn't dare make those concessions from a position of defeat. The strategy did in fact absorb the first shock: the trip to Jerusalem, when it suddenly began to dawn on everybody that something very strange was happening. It was at this point that the whole country began to drown in a profound feeling of futility from which it still hasn't recovered. He could have spared us the war since peace and cooperation with Israel and the United States were his original purpose in waging it in the first place. Neither Israel nor the United States had asked for anything more in 1967 than what he willingly gave them after 1973. But Sadat's fears for his regime turned 'the national war of liberation' into a massacre. The October War was a sound thrashing administered to the people to make

---

14 Some might object to this reading by saying that Nasser obviously had no idea he would die so suddenly. My answer to this objection is that Nasser was already sending implicit messages to this effect to the alliance he was 'fighting'. An example is when he stepped down in 1968 and nominated Zakariyya Muhyildin to take his place. Like all dictators, he was a lot less tenacious than his image suggested.

them swear off all the talk about the nation and its sovereign rights once and for all. The war made it clear that 'the nation' could just as easily gobble up its own children without the slightest concern for their dignity or self-respect. The war did not restore national sovereignty or our rights as citizens; it violated them both in unprecedented ways. Even 'liberated' Sinai, where we were not allowed to move a single soldier without permission, became a whip at our backs: if we refused, they occupied. In the nation that they finally succeeded in forcing to its knees (and not just by way of economic invasion[15]), the only winner was the bourgeoisie. From the 1973 'Victory' on, the simplest of rights became a most expensive commodity.

And so the regime achieved its conditional victory. At the same time, its adversaries warned that a single step further would result in a rout.[16] This forethought on the part of the United States and Israel pointed to the limits of their antagonism to the regime—to their deference even—at the height of the hostilities.[17] But this victory crumbled into dust almost immediately.

---

15 [*Infitah*: the first wave of neoliberal reforms in Egypt.]

16 A message transmitted by [then US secretary of state and national security adviser] Henry Kissinger in a telephone call to Sadat.

17 [For a discussion of Sadat's secret negotiations with Kissinger during and after the October War, see Hazem Kandil, *Soldiers, Spies and Statesmen: Egypt's Road to Revolt* (London: Verso, 2012).]

The struggle for national liberation was crossed out of existence, and the history of this struggle was now to be considered a stupid excess that had to be expiated. The October War was declared to be 'the last war'. Sadat didn't even bother waiting till the cannon had cooled down to wake us up to the fact that he had fought Israel and the United States with soldiers whose blood was dirt cheap, and for no apparent reason other than to reconcile their grieving families to the killers (and this time he did not tearfully choke on his words).[18] We now began an era free of 'national woes', but in the wasteland left behind, the 'euphoria' that Sadat had famously promised us failed to materialize. The 'woes' no longer needed explaining; we forgot—or deliberately ignored —the fact that the national question had not been resolved, and that once again we had become strangers in our own lands. The time when talking about 'the nation' and 'patriotism' elicited contemptuous laughter descended upon our people. But now and then the massive popularity of a silly television spy drama,[19] or the loving pride exhibited at a national-league football game betrayed their old attachments.

And now the pundits have the gall, after having made of humiliation a virtue, to speculate and philosophize and declare their regrets: 'We should have

18 [A reference to the emotional outbursts that Sadat often indulged in during his speeches and public appearances.]

19 [Two famous spy soap operas of the 1980s were *Tears in Shameless Eyes* (1980) and *Ra'fat al-Haggan* (1987).]

surrendered in 1948'! You certainly could have; in fact, that's just what you did the moment you dared, but with the blood of others. Our people are still playing at the game of forgetting, but a time will come when they will remember, for the people are the body of memory.

The student movement was weak because it was forced to confront murky and confused historical conditions (though 'the struggle' seemed at that time so simple and clear), and because it was rooted in an ineffectual and dependent class. This was the (student) petty bourgeoisie; a class that belonged at the time (in its sentiments and in many of its privileges, universal free education being the most important) to the Nasser regime. The historical moment represented a stage in the development of our people's consciousness—a consciousness that had been locked up by Nasser in the prison of childhood minority.

6. *The End*

The students and the masses rose up against the broken promises of the bourgeoisie, but not because they had an alternative set of positions. When the bourgeoisie turned its back on the common cause and the danger became very real, the protests did not grow stronger; instead, everyone suddenly lost their power of speech! This was how the bourgeoisie constantly represented the national struggle and how the role of the masses in defending the regime—morally speaking, of course—came to be defined. People's worst fear was the destruction of the regime at the hands of the country's foreign enemies. The idea that Nasser would have allowed the people to truly participate in the country's military and political affairs is a joke. He had learnt well the lessons of the bourgeois revolutions that threw the doors open to the masses only to collapse in the blink of an eye. This was the same lesson learnt everywhere by the bourgeoisie. Nasser's dictatorship was not 'flawed' as his partisans suppose. On the contrary, he knew exactly where his allegiances lay and which side to choose when the choice became necessary. This is what 'his people' did not understand about him; that he was the original version of 'the benevolent patriarch'[20] (which brings to mind a famous saying about history repeating itself first as tragedy, then as farce). But in all this, the people were as innocent as children. It was not the regime that needed looking after at the time.

The changes were deep and impossible to notice at first—a rapid downward spiral. Those who sold off the country's resources weren't just a handful of outlaws or vultures, but an entire class that until recently

---

20 [Sadat proclaimed himself 'the father of the Egyptian family' and issued the 'Law of Shame' in January 1980 in which an assortment of moral and political 'crimes' became punishable by asset confiscation, blacklisting, internal exile and travel bans.]

had been leading the country in a battle for national independence, monopolizing, even, this leadership and claiming—falsely—the sole merit in so doing.[21] This class, which turned the Egyptian communists into worried mice in their homeland, had eagerly profited from the communist leadership (or at least those who considered themselves communists) in the countries of the socialist camp. Without this support, the Egyptian bourgeoisie would have collapsed from a single blow from the imperialist camp. On whom could it depend after all, when the people were muzzled and the colonizer could not be got rid of with simple charms and incantations? On an army inherited from the colonial era? Every achievement that this class presented to the people as samplings of its generosity rested on the backs of the workers of the socialist states, on the surplus labour which was hardly produced for their own luxury. It was this surplus that built the Egyptian bourgeoisie's army free of charge; an army that it used to patch up its sullied reputation so that it could freely bargain away our dignity and our daily bread.[22]

---

21 [Salih here is describing the 'new class' of technocrats and managers that came into being under Nasser's regime and transitioned into the Sadat regime as the main beneficiaries of market liberalization in Sadat's Open Door years.]

22 [Though a leader of the Non-Aligned Movement, the Nasser regime gravitated increasingly towards the Soviet Union in the 1960s in the form of substantial military and technical aid and

The ultimate blow came from unexpected quarters, and was therefore beyond comprehension. In form and content, it was of an entirely different order than what the people had been taught, through repetition, to expect over the years. The regime was alive and well; no one had hit it on the hand to make it go to Jerusalem as a guest of the Israeli state. On the contrary, this was the climax of its 'victory' (even the Israelis had their suspicions about Sadat's true motives: they put snipers on the roof of the airport). The regime was simply moving 'under the momentum'[23] of seven years of occupation that had taught it some manners. The student movement had shown it a sample of the coming danger, compared with which the danger posed by Israel was nothing. *This* was the truth of the regime, and not the garish fireworks shows that it put on for the people to gape at like awed children nor the tedious nationalist songs that it used to suffocate us. It was the regime's right after all: 'the funeral's in an alley and the departed is a dog,' as the saying goes. Our national liberation was put on fire-sale. The regime settled for 'reclaiming Sinai' when its stated ambition had once been to take the United States itself head on

cultural exchanges. In 1971, Sadat signed a friendship treaty with the Soviet Union. In a sudden move the following year, Sadat summarily expelled all Soviet military advisors from Egypt. The treaty was abrogated in 1976 and relations between the two states severed in 1981.]

23 Sadat's precise description of the October War.

(never mind its apprentice, Israel, the perpetual butt of our great leader's sarcasm). Its own exact words were 'to fight for true national independence and the creation of a vigorous national economy'. What then did the Sinai question have to do with the earthquake that turned the domestic front upside down?

'The preservation of the regime' against the evil conspiracies of colonialism became equivalent to the liberation of Sinai, nothing more—and that, at any price, including the price of selling off our national economy. Sinai was returned, the regime emerged from the crisis unscathed and the economy was sold off on the cheap as the regime's ransom.

This was how the imperative to 'defend' the regime in the name of unquestionable national duty lost its *raison d'être*. But the fabulists didn't seem to notice, including those who opposed Sadat's bargaining strategy (though it really wasn't all that bad for them; hadn't it saved everyone a lot of trouble, his own class first and foremost?). Sadat was at his most honest and apposite and pragmatic when he said that the details were essentially unimportant so long as there were no substantial differences between the bourgeoisie and its strategists over the necessity of making peace with Israel and of opening up our markets to the invasion of foreign capital. These two basic and interdependent principles were at the heart of the whole ruckus. It didn't matter whether Sadat decided to cross the Mitla

Pass[24] or whether he went to Jerusalem or met with the Israelis in Geneva: peace and market liberalization were our manifest destiny because this was exactly what was being prepared for us from 1967 onwards. The October War wasn't fought to change the roadmap of 1967 but to turn it for the first time into a hard reality. It insults our intelligence to be told that it all came to pass as a result of the negotiators' stupidity or miscalculations. Claims like this are the product of the

---

24 [On the evening of the second day of the October War, Egyptian forces held the military advantage in Sinai and were poised to take the strategic Mitla and Gidi Passes, dealing a severe blow to the Israelis and possibly bringing the war to a successful conclusion in the opinion of Egyptian, Israeli and international observers. However, against the urgent and repeated pleas of his senior military command, Sadat refused to advance on the passes and inexplicably halted the offensive on 9 October. Kandil notes that on 8 October, Sadat had sent a secret cable to Kissinger, to assure him that 'Egypt had no intention of intensifying the engagements or widening the confrontation.' Kandil suggests that this blatant betrayal of Egyptian ground forces in Sinai and of the war effort at large was due to Sadat's ambition to curry favour with the United States and to execute his plans to take Egypt into the American camp. Kissinger then informed the Israeli ambassador to Washington of Sadat's pledge to freeze his forces at the passes, which allowed the Israeli army to focus its attention on the Syrian front. (See Kandil, *Soldiers, Spies and Statesmen*, pp. 126–31.) The Egyptian Communist Workers Party put out a paper in 1973 that came to similar conclusions regarding Sadat's real purpose in fighting the October War. See https://goo.gl/ZB9SwE (last accessed on 11 September 2017).]

fake self-delusion of individuals who, unlike Sadat himself, lacked the courage to bear the consequences of the plans they had carefully laid for years. As far as the bourgeoisie was concerned, there was simply no alternative. And when the nightmare overtook them, they quaked in their boots. The making of this history required an insufferable level of corruption and contemptibility on the part of the intellectuals who worked as the regime's propagandists and who lost their shadows the moment 'the great leader and teacher'[25] passed away. Sadat served his class in the best way possible in light of its non-existent choices. He was the ideal representative of the bourgeoisie and its interests in the era of its degeneration, just as Nasser had been its leader when its star was rising. Anyone who pretends that nothing changed in the meantime is utterly deceived as to the new reality of the Egyptian 'national' bourgeoisie. These people have their heads in the clouds (as it used to please their writers to describe us Marxists with the easygoing tolerance of the strong for the weak); they longingly gaze back at the good old times that are lost for ever. 'Would that the days of youth return!' said the poet.[26] Today you will find these individuals busy rifling through their old papers.

The masses had failed to flex their muscles in order to change the status quo. Instead, they served as

25 [That is, Nasser.]

26 [From the Diwan of the eighth-century Arab poet Abu al-'Atahiyya.]

human fuel for a war of whose true purpose they were innocent. The bourgeoisie and its ideologues concurred that it would be out of the question to allow them any say in such matters, and everything else was mere detail and small change ill suited to the heroics of useless opposition—useless because the opposition was incapable of changing facts on the ground, only of making retroactive and futile adjustments in the jigsaw puzzle of the peace negotiations. The planners of these negotiations are now busy policing the order they brought into being. To them, 'the public', far from representing a potential source of dissent, is nothing but an applauding audience. They belong to that category known as the passive masses. This is their proper place and station (for our melancholy intellectual is the type that respects 'station' more than he likes to admit). They certainly cannot be expected to impose a revision of the maps since this requires managerial arts that only parvenus like our hypothetical friend, the intellectual, can command . . . and may God help us all.

The occasional 'objection' to the status quo can never whitewash individuals whose famed pens worked tirelessly over the years to excuse all manner of crimes. The day has come for those who drew endless amusement from observing the opposition playing at the margins of events to drink from the same cup (if only they hadn't spit in it first). They too might trace

their genealogy to a consumptive, half-starved opposition. As for 'the glorious past,' the reckoning of it will
be harsh indeed in a better future than the moment
we at present inhabit—that is, if it is even remem-
bered by generations who will hopefully have happier
and more useful things to do. The age of 'patriotism'
celebrated by all these types of intellectuals and bourgeois leaders came to an end at the same time as the
era when the national struggle paid its bills out of Cold
War coffers. These 'patriots' played the strings of the
conflict in a dirty game directed against all parties,
especially against the masses in whose name they
played. That time is over now; the time when they
were able to play all sides and effortlessly steal all the
gains—including the halo of patriotism and honour—
with nothing but their 'art' of crisis management. We
have now reached a moment when mixing up religion
and politics isn't going to be enough to reclaim the
nation's dignity and that of its citizens. Maybe this is
the only real advantage of looking back through a dark
glass rather than the rose-tinted variety.

7. *The Age of 'Endings' Isn't Over*
Could the students have held on during a transition of
this magnitude? They were confronted by a class long
used to monopolizing authority and the right to speak,
think and act—a class that was taking an entire society

with it into the abyss. With no independent footing to help keep its balance, it was inevitable that the society as a whole would fall with this class, that it would pay yet again the price of this class' initial attack on its freedom when its star was on the rise. The first exorbitant bill took the form of the regime's famous 'gifts' in education, healthcare and self-respect that were handed out on the revolution's successive anniversaries. Meanwhile, the students are now busy looking for work.

The student movement would not have suddenly found itself at the very centre of political life had this not been a temporary, transitional moment. We had not yet been divided into killers and victims; divisions that have meanwhile multiplied to include the nation's religious minorities and make them feel like strangers in their own country. Now that the bourgeoisie has taken us to the last stretch of the dead end it created, now that it has brought us to this dark period in our history, the conflict has entered a completely new phase that is much more brutal than the one which the students managed to lead in an era that is forever gone. Only God himself can know how we will be able to escape this new place. The laws that governed the eruption of revolutions through the beginning of the twentieth century have changed, as has the composition of the various social classes and their relative

power. International capitalism seems to have learnt
the lessons of those early revolutions better than everyone else and, with its vast resources, has become practically the sole architect of this dark era. The only
stable exception to this rule was made by the peoples
of the socialist states. And yet we still don't know if
they will manage to take the next step in shaping their
history. Will they succeed? Will they be abandoned to
their own devices this time too?[27] How will this choke-
hold ever come loose, so that we ourselves may dare
to breathe? This is the question for which there are as
yet no clear answers. But when the answers start to
come, they won't remain a secret. The only certainty
is that if we do not struggle to liberate our country
from neocolonialism we will never be free within its
borders.

This is why today's students are quite different
from those of yesterday—a difference that is representative of changing realities inside the university gates.
Sharp lines of wealth and poverty divide students
today and the only thing they have in common is
the profound feeling of ruin that haunts the entire
country. The rich among them take drugs and drown

---

27 The middle classes are on the rise all over the world. Their
ideas, lifestyles and even their dreams are shaped by the handful of capitalists who have convinced them that they are the
ones who govern. In the socialist states, the emerging middle
class looks quite similar to its former rulers. They too dream of
blue jeans and cassette recorders and they despise the poor.

themselves in the vapid pop music of the day in the hope of filling up the empty spaces in their souls. The poor find refuge in religion in search of inner strength to fend off the crushing burdens and insecurities of their lives. Today, those who are politically active bear no resemblance to the noisy, light-hearted leaders of the 1970s. They are people with stern faces and long, unkempt beards who grimly proclaim their boorish, inflated identities.[28] Instead of copies of student papers, they carry knives and chains to fight off the humiliations dished out to them by a society that ignores their misery. Their violence is new to us but familiar to nations that have experienced devastating economic hardship. This violence is called fascism. Over the past couple of decades, significant sectors of the petty bourgeoisie—historically, and with few exceptions, an important base of the Egyptian nationalist and democratic movement—have been won over to the practice of violence. They cannot change our collective situation; they can only give it a fascist tint if, God forbid, they were ever to come to power.

---

28 [In the mid-1970s, the Sadat regime began to use Islamist student groups to harass and intimidate the leftist political organizations active on campus. These groups came to dominate student politics in the 1980s and '90s thanks to an expanding base, the effectiveness of their violent tactics and strategic collaboration with the regime. See Kamal Khalil's memoir: *Hikayat min zaman fat* (Stories from a Past Era) (Cairo: Bayt al-Yasmin, 2013).]

The student movement was born at the end of an era. It was destined to turn the page on a cherished, expiring past and to usher in a new and oppressive historical moment. It missed the opportunity of opening up a real path to independence for our people—and maybe this was exactly what was never meant to be in the first place.

8. *Conclusion of the Two Stories from One Trench*

When the bourgeoisie finally decided on its course of action and, exploiting the war's 'momentum', radically transformed the state's socialist and nationalist direction, there was no political force to oppose it on the ground.[29] The student movement evaporated along with the new possibilities it had brought into being, and its leaders found themselves out in the cold, condemned to taste the same contempt they had heaped on the generation of the sixties. They too had become leaders without followers. We came to know the meaning of fatigue and despair. We witnessed the 'betrayal' of Marxist thought and the celebration of the most noxious ideas to come out of the declining bourgeoisie's bag of tricks. We too were crushed by the wheel of historical transition. We thought it was *our*

---

29 [Salih here uses the Arabic word *maydan*—battlefield, square, ground—in an implicit reference to the sites of public struggle, i.e. *maydan al-tahrir*, the iconic location of the 1971–72 student uprising and the uprising of 2011.]

time and that we would change it, but we could not see clearly enough the ground on which our feet stood. It became apparent—yet again—that the time of true leaders had not yet come. In either case, the people remained defenceless, as did their intellectuals and militants. Heroes do not emerge in the absence of epics.

But the story continues.

CHAPTER TWO

The Afterlives of the Student-Movement Generation

I came to love a written word I found
Its letters glittered and shone with a glare
I wanted to keep it in my heart, it cried: Beware,
Every heart I entered broke without a sound!

Salah Jahin

1. *An Appendix to the Story of Two Generations*

During the Nasser era, leftists with real talent engaged in a circumscribed literary movement whose parameters were defined by the regime. It forced them to speak in symbols and metaphors. It instilled in them a permanent sense of persecution and feelings of guilt that weren't always personal in nature. As for the half-talented ones, they lounged in the coffeehouses with nothing to do but chew on bitter defeat and criticize the talented ones—until God blessed them with the student movement.

These 'revolutionary intellectuals' thought of themselves the vanguard of the Egyptian working class, the entire Egyptian people even. But it was a vanguard rejected by its would-be followers who were on an entirely different wavelength, living victory after victory on the coattails of Nasser, the great leader, and regarding them—when it bothered to look at them at all—as a breed of rare animal. The inability to act effectively—to interact in any way at all with a hostile reality—mangled these militants alive. Their brains and the shelves of their bookcases were crowded with 'radical' ideas that had no consistent, principled application in the world around them. The only thing these ideas were good for was to patch together a shining image of personal militancy propped up by abstract political positions and the occasional prison sentence. And even then, the title of 'militant' wasn't enough to satisfy the bloated egos of these individuals. Nothing less than the status of 'leader' could shore up the humiliated pride of an 'intellectual' wrapped up in his personal tragedy rather than the tragedy of his people.

The student movement presented these intellectuals with the solution to a long-running existential problem: that of their own superfluity. It might have offered a small window of opportunity for their deliverance if only they hadn't already spent a good part of their lives doing absolutely nothing. Their lives were shaped by the dichotomy between a Marxism forged at a time of international revolutionary advances whose language was one of strength and optimism (and transformed by the Soviet regime into a religion that brooked no opposition), and a defeat—or a full-on assault—that didn't even permit the defeated the dignity of a good fight. The same regime that took the people hostage in exchange for a few temporary political gains placed these revolutionary intellectuals in a quixotic bind when it turned them into a minority hounded and persecuted by the people themselves. As such, they were forced either to cooperate with the regime or to waste away in some forgotten corner where their ideas weren't worth much more than their very real paralysis. The tragedy of this situation wasn't just about their inability to continue the struggle. The sharpest blow of all was their total alienation from the sentiments of an entire people all turned towards the external enemy—a people lacking even the slightest desire to liberate itself. The constant harping on 'revolutionary optimism' in the writings of some of these intellectuals fed back into the same duplicity that governed their lives and produced a gaping hole in their vision. Sometimes their critical analysis of bourgeois thought was penetrating, and even inspiring. It was much less so when they wrote about the masses, so precious to them and yet so foreign. In the real-world situation, where both the popular movement and its revolutionary 'leaders' were paralysed, their writing about the masses was misleading and distorted because their optimism was quite simply a sham. It was a bookish optimism that scornfully ignored the tragic experience processed by an alienated sensibility. Their alienation crept into the deepest core of their social and personal relationships and infected them with the worst of bourgeois values ('worst' because the bourgeoisie itself was not yet disintegrating at this point while they themselves were). The upbeat revolutionary ideals that took over the international socialist movement (especially the literary movement) were the creation of writers-for-hire whose social realism was therefore suspect, regardless of its elegance or skill, stylistic or otherwise. This was not the optimism (or pessimism) of writers who had found their own way—in a different time and place—to their professed beliefs, but of those who took refuge from 'heresy' in the absolutism of a fixed and ideological understanding of an abstract model, in ideas that became the vertebra of a twisted intellectual coherence. They were incapable of discovering any kind of real bridge between this twisted structure and their reality. So, to complete the irony, it was 'faith' that offered the petty bourgeois a suitable alternative to the truth of his world—a truth that didn't always guarantee adequate compensation for his rebellion.

For them, time was a turbid, stagnant current while for the people, full of hope and confidence, it rippled with life and vitality. It was as though these luckless intellectuals observed the masses through the glass of a jar in which they were trapped. Nothing in their lives had prepared them to fight off time's dispassionate claws. The extent of the damage done to the student movement by the poisonous pond scum that floated to the surface in this environment was not entirely clear until these former 'leaders' finally acquired a real following and commanded the destinies of real human beings.

When the student movement exploded onto the political stage in ways that were unprecedented during the decades of Nasserist hegemony, the unemployed old-guard leaders took heart. This, they believed, was their springboard to 'the socialist struggle'. Now that the people had begun to awaken from the nightmare of bourgeois mystification, now that deliverance was in sight, it seemed to them their time had come. They would finally stretch their legs and mount the attack after all those years spent hanging around in cafes. On this orphan student movement, they placed their last bets. But the bourgeoisie had one more trick up its sleeve before dragging everyone along to the grave that would gather the mortal remains of an entire era. For one last time, as it breathed its last (truly this time!), the bourgeoisie pulled the rug out from under them (again). And when? At the very moment when their long-cherished fantasy of becoming a force to be reckoned with in the real world seemed to be on the point of realization—that real world that had constantly eluded the scope of their enlightened ideas and condemned their misguided revolutionary optimism to oblivion. After the October War and the critical historical transformation that came in its wake, there was no significant broad-based struggle for these intellectuals to lead.

The student movement itself produced a negligible string of inconsequential leaders and disappeared without leaving any other trace. This next generation of leaders was now left bewildered: contrary to their dearest expectations, they had become the surplus junk of an era that had taught them nothing, in a new world that they could barely recognize. Having no idea what to do with themselves, they turned their attention elsewhere. Meanwhile, awaiting their 'deliverance', the old guard who had composed the movement out of nothing, began to play the Stalinist vanguard game with the students—a strategy that offered the perfect compensation for a past without real struggle, only oppression and exploitation.

The student movement attracted a following of petty-bourgeois leftists. As such, they were well matched to their unemployed leaders: lions of the same pride. Those leaders finally found their long-sought object in a group of children who still hadn't learnt to walk, but who nonetheless believed themselves to be the natural vanguard of the Egyptian people. And why not? The masses were, after all, out there on the streets in their thousands, heartily repeating their chants. The leaders of the student movement were young men in their early twenties who had memorized a few Marxist phrases and whose self-appointed mission filled them with a naive arrogance for which they would soon pay a steep price. The fact that they were surrounded by the spent Marxist leadership of the Nasser era resulted in a jolly farce that would surely reduce the audience to tears of laughter and repulsion were all its chapters to be narrated. The victims of this farce were destroyed beyond repair by shame and bitterness.[1]

Well before the Egyptian people split into warring classes, the student-movement generation had broken up into cliques and factions: the extreme left, the right wing of the left and everything in-between. There was no material basis for the general loathing and the constant accusations exchanged by the various factions because these were splits that didn't in any way represent external realities. Nor did they reflect choices or positions coming from the masses, which were united around the single demand for the recovery of the nation's sovereignty. Far from owing their origins to strategic differences over how to deal with the disposition of the masses, the splits were merely disputes that had spilt out from Nasser's prisons. The communists of the sixties generation took different positions on the Nasser regime and on a host of other questions besides. Not all of these positions were worthy of respect, emerging as they did from a cloistered clique of leftists ravaged by the Defeat of 1967. Instead of leaving us to our own devices—of giving us the space to work out our living reality and to let experience sift

---

1 There are exceptions for every generation, of course. These are known to everyone and command respect.

out left from right—they nursed us on their poisoned milk. These prior internecine conflicts had devastating consequences. The student movement inherited them before the real world could shape its growth, because certain individuals deliberately moulded a handful of people into material with which to settle old scores. These individuals were shameless enough to treat their 'disciples' as though they were a contested family legacy: dunce apprentices for ready-made teachers who had never learnt how to be men.

It's no surprise then that the positions of all the factions within the student movement were characterized by doctrinal rigidity, from the 'extreme left' to the 'extreme right'. The sixties generation didn't have the popular base to make it a force for real change or to put its claims to the test (their militants were famous for their citation of texts; one of the bad habits we learnt from them) or, at the very least, to force them do anything else besides constantly argue! Our generation inherited this deadening aptitude for endless arguing from people who had nothing but time on their hands. This habit of ours actually became a substitute for productive work. It even became a substitute for the possibility of human communication thanks to the arrogance of bloated egos.

On top of all this, Egyptian Marxists of the 1960s were children of the Cold War and of the Stalinism which had transformed Marxism into an official religion. In the realm of ideas, 'truth' took on a single,

absolute face, with an official spokesperson, an absolute in himself, the representative of authority and of
a hierarchy in which the credibility of truth and even
the right to a perspective on truth decreased the further down the base one descended. When even the
communist parties in countries with a deep-rooted
history of labour struggle and democracy (the Western
European countries, for example) were moulded along
the pattern set by Moscow, what then of our countries,
which never had a strong, independent labour movement worthy of the name?

The Marxists of the 1960s were 'Stalinists by
inclination', including those who considered themselves to be on the left of Soviet revisionism (the
expression itself is religious in the same measure that
it lacks courage). This was because the only 'successful' communist venture (i.e. of taking and holding
power) was characterized by obvious fascist elements.
Even the most far-left of these Marxists didn't dare
allow themselves to consider that something at the
core of the socialist experiment was very wrong. How
amazing that they only started to worry about the
future of socialist countries with no democratic labour
movements, when these regimes were directly threatened by the entry of the labour movements onto the
political stage! Only then did our Marxists rise to the
occasion and declare 'socialism' to be 'in danger'. And
those who had debased the concept of 'historical necessity' so they could use it as an excuse for Stalin's crimes

suddenly forgot what it meant when they heaped all the blame on one man for the rot that threatened to bring the Soviet regime toppling down after 70 years of socialism (this was when the million-dollar question was: Are you with Gorbachev or against him?). In short, these people were incapable of thinking about the history of socialism or its future without anchoring it in state power, and this in spite of the absolute and equivocal deification of 'the people' in their political literature. All this was nothing but the depressing fantasy of 'revolutionary optimists'. If our Marxists had cared at all for the peoples of the Soviet Bloc, they would at least have had some sympathy for them instead of their smug satisfaction at the spectacle of hardship they endured with the creeping invasion of Western capital (our Marxists actually hoped that these tribulations would chasten them back into the fold of the only kind of socialism they were able to imagine!). But the petty-bourgeois position towards authority is sentimental and non-negotiable: all of them know their instructions by heart.

The continuing existence of the Soviet regime was the only remaining source of this pious certitude that had once been inspired by a huge international wave of worker revolutions in the capitalist West. The wave retreated, the glow of the first victorious socialist revolution disintegrated behind the iron curtain and the bourgeois national-liberation movements of the third world—whose successes were built on the ruins of the communist movements—came to occupy the centre stage of world events. In view of what they suffered at the hands of the Nasser regime, the Egyptian communists' position towards the Soviet state was like that of 'the bald woman who boasts of her niece's luxurious hair'. They colluded in the mistakes that cost the Soviet people dear—mistakes they dismissed as 'tendentious Western propaganda'. They weren't a bit worried about the future of socialism so long as it remained in power and ruled with an iron fist. Then when the creeping rot made the entire edifice that had been built and maintained through great sacrifice crumble to pieces, the only thing they managed to pull out of their bag of Marxist theory were accusations against Mikhail Gorbachev.

This was the affective disorder of the 1960s left as well as of our generation of 'stepchildren', from the extreme left to the extreme right.[2] A Stalinist god was better than a thousand theories of consensus building. One of the predictable ironies of this situation is that many among our generation are now reassessing the whole socialist project (now that it's lost state power, of course). It isn't clear whether this is because they no longer believe in the Marxist critique of capitalist society (or have found a more effective political theory

---

2 The 'bureaucratic left' was of course an exception, used as it was to useful comradely relations with the Soviet bureaucracy. For them, anyone at the head of this bureaucracy was always right.

to do the job) or whether they consider its vision of a classless society to be a fraud. Whatever the case, the theory has been liberated from its devotees and perhaps might now live again for the first time in decades as a result.

The Marxism of the sixties generation was a Marxism of insular intellectuals deprived of imagination and trampled on by the real world. They didn't dare challenge the dominant doctrinal rigidity, which was a sign of the profound crisis in the conditions of class struggle the world over. They refused to acknowledge the crisis of Marxism because they were mesmerized by the glamour of the Soviet experience. They could not imagine a world free of Cold War divisions (whose ultimate collapse opened the door to class struggle, even if this happened first in the socialist states) nor could they think beyond the Soviet regime's authoritarian attitude towards art and literature—and history, of course. This was first and foremost an attitude of obligatory dishonesty, and it was visible in the relationship of the 'vanguard' to anyone with the grave misfortune of falling under its influence—from the rank-and-file to the masses.

The Stalinism of the sixties generation delayed our understanding of the farce that turned us into their playthings. Alliances that were supposed to be voluntary between militants struggling to liberate the world were transformed into master–slave relations that, in the late stages, came to closely resemble the structure of religious brotherhoods. The concept of the 'elite' who bring 'enlightenment' to the masses took a fascist turn. There was no real basis for the imaginary distinction they made between themselves and the masses and it only served to isolate them further. In the minds of these professional leaders, the masses became mere featureless blocs—yet another hollow and endlessly repeated mantra that the members of this elect tribe bandied back and forth between them so as to give the appearance of consensus between people astonishingly incapable of dialogue. Having become an isolated clique—completely ignorant of everything connected to the people's real lives—from their daily struggles and their strategies for making ends meet, to the temptations of life in capitalist society, their activism lost all meaning. It was as though they were actors in a play who collude in convincing one another that the action is real. And so the debates raged on for no real reason other than the intellectual whims of the debaters. Doctrinal and political polemics became the only real excuse for their existence. Their debates became increasingly scholastic (the 'class transformation' of social groups they had never come in contact with; comparisons between 'militant tactics' that only a prophet of theory could pronounce upon) while the masses remained silent.

No militant who is ignorant of how people actually live can decide for them how they should conduct their struggles or what they should be prepared to do. A wide cross-section of Egyptians had already begun to change their political thinking—the entire direction of their spiritual lives even—before we militants began to realize that something unexpected was happening. We were too busy with the fierce arguments that split us into competing groups and factions. We transformed the revolution into a long waking dream lacking all joy. Illusion became the fabric from which we knit our understanding of the world and of our place in it; illusion propped up by a hard core of memories of the movement before it had lost the real ground from which to test the truth of its deeds. Over the years, bands of young men put themselves within reach of the merciless claws of the police, living the lives of outlaws and willingly sacrificing the possibility of a future in the workaday world. Some of them were gifted with real talent in other spheres, yet they chose to live and work in penurious, sometimes inhuman, conditions. They executed feats of wonder in order to meet in secret but these meetings became a kind of prison of their own making: a strange, parallel life with its own language, its own rhythms and responsibilities, its own musings and worries—a weird and studiously constructed freedom that served no purpose. In this bizarre isolation, they read works on revolution from the previous century. They endlessly parsed their alienation with appropriately intelligent observations. A credulous sense of their own distinction made them drain the cup of their estrangement and still thirst for more. They set up their laws—laws that claimed the power to love and hate, to anoint and depose, to loose and bind. This private world turned society into an 'outside' place; a place of 'us' versus 'them' where we were the strangers. In our forced dealings with this outside world, we put on disguises in order to appear 'normal': 'professions' we didn't profess, 'ordinary' occupations that were only important to us insofar as they allowed us to preach our message, false ideological identities even, all the things that make up an observable existence, that allow people to live together and come to know one another. But we were only ever our true selves in each other's company, far from the world. A fine truth indeed.

All kinds of prodigious marvels flourished in that phantasmagorical world. Dwarfs were transformed into giants and cheap comedies became fatal tragedies. Grand sacrifices were exploited to satisfy twisted caprices, and intimate friendships were born—love affairs even—between people who were incapable of truly knowing each other. The idle talk of neurotic imaginations acquired the power of conviction, momentous events created coincidences, some of which were amusing, others obscene. All this and more became possible in this artificial world, which was infinitely more distorted than any reality. And so, when we finally walked out into the light of day, the devastation was total. We were like mummies crumbling to dust in the sunlight. It was difficult for many to make peace with themselves after everything that had happened. The world that they stepped into was hardly more merciful than the one they'd left behind. For some, apostasy was the easiest way to regain the balance. Those who weren't able to kick the addiction to their own self-importance merely soldiered on by moving into different circles (international 'humanitarian' organizations, for example) even though they had to calmly bury their past in a forgotten corner in order to start their new lives.

This was what vanguardism did to our generation. Becoming a member of the 'vanguard' was the first step on the road to disengagement from the real world and it generated alienated relationships of all kinds. It was an elite that devoured itself. Its obsession with hierarchy fostered so much rivalry and hatred, fear and sycophancy, that one was astonished to remember that these people had once been rebels.

One of the coarsest forms the hierarchy took was the division between 'authors' and everyone else—the drudges who did the heavy lifting and who were also the most likely to be captured by the police. To be counted a writer was considered a prestigious and unquestionable value. From these heights you could terrorize everyone with reams of paper that no one but you had the right to judge. Everyone else's role was simply to interpret and to defend if necessary, like good little disciples. The status of 'writer' meant you'd joined the ranks of the super-elite—the creators who set the direction; the 'minds' that direct those who 'do'. The other side of this coin was that militants who weren't inclined to write or to claim the genius of intellectual authority were supposed to consider themselves defective in some sense, lacking the one accomplishment that mattered in their circles. So it was only natural that the number of authors increased exponentially, and that the real builders and organizers —those unsung heroes of any living political movement and its beating heart—wasted away. If only they had had the courage to think for themselves. They would have realized that the writing was mediocre at best, and they would have rejected it, before it became too late—a militancy that ends up degrading real militants. The truth is, not a single one of those distinguished writers managed to become a recognized author when they moved back into the real world.[3] Besides which, this division of labour and the distinction between thinkers and militants that it produced was literally duplicated from capitalist society. A similar logic governs the vanguardist attachment to 'the great leader'. In the closed sects that the militant inhabits, the leader is a sheikh and a mufti. Everyone hangs on his every eloquent pronouncement, his

---

3 This observation applies to the writers who belonged to the student movement and does not include the political theorists of the sixties.

sacred babble, even where their personal relationships are concerned. Absolute obedience is a principle, and those who disagree are 'heretics' who deserve execution (for now, in the figurative sense only, of course). The leader's rights are unlimited. It comes as no surprise then that his anointed heirs will be hustlers who enjoy the thrill of dominating minds trained to submission and intellectual and spiritual servility.

This last point deserves closer attention. Children do not remain children for ever and there comes a time when adulthood forces an accounting. The relationship of these young men and women to the world of ideas in general, and to Marxism in particular, was limited. They suddenly found themselves playing the role of leaders of the Egyptian people before learning the simple facts of life and were consequently trapped between the rock and the hard place of arrogance and ineptitude. They didn't have enough integrity and honesty to admit they weren't up to it and they weren't able to do the job. They needed a miracle. The only solution to this dilemma was to play at being leader and hand themselves over lock, stock and barrel to mentors whose only claim to militancy was having once spent a bit of time in prison. These persons were incapable of leading a nanny goat. Having practically stumbled upon their victims, they had the impudence to act as enlightened gurus who had solved all the thorny dilemmas of the struggle. This was no miracle; it was a catastrophe that decisively led an entire generation to its doom and a fate shared across the entire spectrum of the 1970s student left. The movement was exploited by a generation deeply tainted by its experience during the Nasser regime. Fools really do deserve to be ridden by scoundrels.

2. On the Different Roads Taken

The people upstairs and the people downstairs:

In the old days, intellectuals belonged to the propertied classes, back when these classes were supported by a rich patrimony and storied traditions. When the intellectuals rebelled against the spiritual death of their class with no alternative in sight, they turned wild. This is what happens to Grigory Alexandrovitch Pechorin in Mikhail Lermontov's masterpiece, *A Hero of Our Time*. Pechorin is noble, handsome, supremely haughty, even towards death. His illusions about his class are shattered; he abandons it to the profligacy and gossip of its St Petersburg drawing rooms and takes himself off on a one-way journey across the vast tundra of Russia to search for something that is truly alive. He imagines he has found this thing in the form of a Tatar girl whose language he does not know and who is separated from him by centuries of backwardness. The game of love—always threatened by happy endings—fails to slake his thirst, so he takes to flirting with death, a shortcut through the tortuous maze of experience. With the melancholy passing of every experience coloured by hope or illusion that fails to offer salvation, his spiritual death is gradually accomplished, and he makes his last voyage to an alien land (Persia) where his alienation becomes complete and where he dies, alone, of malaria.

The sons of the modern propertied classes are different (perhaps even more so in the countries of the third world). Nasser put an end to 'exploitative capital' and created a new bourgeoisie composed of members of the class he was born into—the petty bourgeoisie. They would become the masters of 'socialist' Egypt and the political and economic spine of its army, and they were bound to Nasser and his regime by powerful ties of loyalty. Death had mercy on the man. He never lived to see with his own eyes and hear with his own ears his once-loyal soldiers complaining in their counsels about 'state intervention' in the private sector (in the form of 'socialist' funds, of course) and baring their fangs in newspaper columns about his 'age of dictatorship'.[4] It was an age that no one any longer had a kind word for, except those who benefitted least from it (lucrative franchises, proximity to authority and to the sources of free money were only available to the select few, after all) and those who really had been destroyed by a dictatorship that stripped them of every

4 [Salih is referring to the Nasser-era bureaucrats and officers who seamlessly made the transition into the Sadat regime and profited from the Open Door.]

means of self-defence. These are the Egyptians who were defeated without a single shot being fired when the savage attack of the Open Door came upon them. They are the ones who still remember Nasser as having sold them a dream of dignity (theirs and the nation's, in the days when both came to the same thing) and they were sorely deceived.

In Nasser's day, this new bourgeoisie was neither storied nor homogenous. It was a hodgepodge of all the various strands of the petty bourgeoisie that is so extensive in our country. Naturally, those who rose in the ranks of the regime hastily repudiated their class origins. This is why you'll find extended families half of whom sit high up close to the summit while the other half languish below with 'the people': the brother a minister and the uncle a nightwatchman. The social imagination of the one half is constituted by images of fancy clubs and holidays in European capitals; the other half draws on warm recollections of intimate back alleys, improvised neighbourhood football matches and merry thug-life (but this past is made up of bits and pieces of a social map that has disappeared, and which is better forgotten). The one half acts in power and people listen closely when they talk; the other half are awash in petty-bourgeois contradictions—they shake in fear of authority and they dream of climbing to the top while somehow keeping their hands clean. Nasser's regime really did offer its minions an almost ideal solution to these contradictions. They enjoyed all the privileges of power offered by the regime, but they were also proudly able to claim service to the national struggle and a 'socialist' one to boot. The balancing act didn't last long though. They eventually grew big enough in their offices to see the world through the eyes of the bourgeoisie, which has no need of principles to justify its behaviour, especially its economic behaviour. When the Open Door arrived, they had acquired enough 'flexibility' to profit extensively from it. They quickly learnt that 'investment has no religion'.[5] What had recently been a socialist economy was now a market open to any and every kind of investment, from foreign to Salafi. Every one of them went about choosing

---

5 The expression is taken from Dr Fouad Zakariyya in an article from *Al-Ahram* about the tragedy of Al-Rayyan. [The Rayyan scandal was a 1980s Islamic investment scheme that defrauded middle-class Egyptians of 3 billion pounds and wiped out their savings. The money was smuggled abroad with the assistance of various regime politicians, journalists and new celebrity preachers. The money, of course, disappeared and some of these partners were sorely disappointed. The trial of Ahmad Al-Rayyan (who had appeared out of nowhere, taken on the persona of a devout 'new Muslim' and quickly amassed a vast fortune) took place in 1989. He received a 15-year sentence, but the Interior Ministry extended his detention for a few more years and he spent most of the next two decades in and out of prison, hounded by the shady network of backers bent on reclaiming 'their' money. The corruption and venality of the affair made an indelible mark on the national psyche and marked a milestone of sorts in the political economy of post-1952 Egypt.]

whichever brand suited their new ideological prefer-
ences. But it was all the same in the end: an exercise
in cold-blooded opportunism.

Nonetheless, Nasser's mandarins held on to their
old-new class pride. They considered themselves
respectable, different in kind and vastly superior to the
'vermin' of the Open Door. They were really bothered
by the social origins of these newly minted million-
aires. But the laws of the market don't distinguish
between the garbage collector or the porter and the late
petty bourgeois. All these former socialists could never
wrap their minds around this aspect of bourgeois
'democracy'—its rules of equity, one might say. Their
deep-rooted respect for hierarchy, with its mystification of 'the upper classes' (and they must be the last
ones to 'arrive', of course) still ran deep in their veins.
What right did they have to look down their noses at
the millionaire garbage collectors[6] when their own
existence as a class was also based on expropriation
and pillage? They were the principal beneficiaries of
the regime's seizure of the property of the big
landowners and capitalists after all—of the expropriation of their clubs, rest-houses, etc., of their authority[7]

---

6 [The pillage of the Open Door was conducted by a consor-
tium of well-placed regime players and savvy up-and-coming
brokers and businessmen. They were known in popular language as 'the fat cats'.]

7 [Salih is referring here to the wave of Nasser-era nationalizations in the 1950s and '60s.]

(all propertied classes are afflicted with amnesia when it comes to the question of how they amassed their wealth). Their only edge was the 'principles' that gave the cover of legitimacy to their thieving. They had hitched their social climbing to an ambitious nationalist–capitalist project ('socialist' according to Nasser) but then they just washed their hands of the whole affair and of Nasser himself as though both were a kind of scabies (and they know that they can't deceive history for ever). They even 'discovered' that their antagonism towards colonialism had been the source of all our miseries, since it had turned out to be so costly. I don't find it at all surprising that they themselves pulled down the whole edifice that had propped them up as a class in the first place. They executed Sadat's orders to the letter, as his 'socialist' predecessor had trained them to do, at all the fateful moments. Even the dissidents didn't forget to take their money with them to invest abroad. Far and wide they announced the end of great dreams and the beginning of the age of 'realism', where there are no dreams, no purpose, no meaning to life apart from material gain—the source of safety and security, the grand prize in a nightmarish collective struggle to survive.

The new Nasserist bourgeoisie was a slave to property in all its forms: high-ranking posts and positions, and profound respect for class status—everything, in short, that the bourgeois revolutions supposedly set out to replace with democratic class relations. Their class composition also explains the temperament and behaviour of their offspring, when their militant project disintegrated.[8] They didn't go crazy or turn ascetic or become alcoholics (though some in fact did) and they didn't have to sell themselves to escape spiralling downward mobility (though they practised the obscene luxury of condemning those who did). Property was their lifeline. These former militants found the same institutions they had rebelled against waiting to embrace them with open arms: a family to protect them and give them financial support, a close-knit patronage network offering all kinds of opportunities for work and travel, the comfort and respect guaranteed by belonging to a flourishing and prosperous social group and countless little luxuries to make up for the past. But this process unfolded on a different basis than it did for their parents. In the lives of these young men and women, social distinction came to replace political distinction. They moved back into defined class positions and began to draw former comrades into their new orbit. From the heights of these positions and the centre of their commodious networks, their zones of luxury, they courted men and women whom they chose from among the poorest of the generation's 'gifted' individuals—artists who were able to create works of real value in some field or other,

8 [The children of Nasser's 'new class' being the student-movement militants of the 1970s.]

or to shine, talent or not, in some capacity, be it nothing more than providing quality entertainment at their lavish and 'progressive' entertainments. Court-jester types are always attracted to these kinds of gatherings, and not even for advantage necessarily but just because luxury is an end in itself. Nobody deliberately set out to create this situation. It just came into being with the force of cold reality. Yesterday's political rivals, with all their various strategic and tactical differences, were at least partners in a struggle that seemed for a while to be capable of creating a small community 'liberated' from the overbearing and oppressive laws of society. But when that common ground crumbled, relations between former comrades came to rest on the one basis that now governed all existing social relationships, the 'pragmatic' basis: class hierarchy.

These rival social cliques sprang up spontaneously, but they quickly produced their own stable instruments of domination. All parties concerned were fully aware of the constant bargaining taking place, and the way people acted as a result became increasingly crude. For example, social obeisance became a 'right' that the young bourgeois patrons demanded everyone respect and they occasionally made a show of power by publically forcing the issue. A silent struggle for celebrity began between the various actors in this drama, to the point where the cliques acquired names just like political parties. It goes without saying that personal relationships inside these cliques (which were more fanatical than any political party) were devoured by rivalry and envy, bitterness and calculation. These were the signs of utter ruin. From now on, everyone understood that a shared past struggle would not be a guarantee of basic ethical relationships in the future.

Meanwhile, the former petty-bourgeois militants who were overtaken by the social train as it sped on towards increasingly sharp class polarization tried to find some stable ground under their feet (it was clear now that their dreams of liberation weren't all they had lost). And because this was no longer the 1960s (a time when it was possible to live on next to nothing and when you didn't need to be a militant to feel alive in a world seething with change, with intellectual vitality and political optimism, both at home and abroad) the search for moral and material security ended for some of them in ways that the intellectuals of the sixties could never have dreamt of: brokerage and bucket-shop businesses, for example, or membership in openly fascist parties that offered a quick move up the ladder and guaranteed social acceptance. Then, of course, there was the Gulf media industry that sucked up anyone with even a modicum of talent and turned them into petrodollar culture-hucksters. If it weren't for the bitterness of it all, the spectacle of this former militant petty bourgeois scurrying up the social ladder to join the ranks of 'respectable' and highly remunerative institutions (public and corporate research councils, government office; marriage) would be quite amusing. From these new perches, they defended themselves by ruthlessly pouring contempt on their past political positions. You might hear one of them, for example, attacking with pointed ferocity Lenin's naive attempt to impose wage equality between 'professionals' and workers. Another one trains himself to speak in the manner of 'respectable people'—a lazy drawl completely opposite to the way he used to talk, when his speech was clipped and tense. The strange thing is that the ones who used to be the most radical militants were the most eager to rush off in the opposite direction in their defeat. We learnt that 'radicalism' wasn't the automatic badge of integrity some of us thought it was back in the day. Ideas had brought us together—or so we thought—but in reality, as we fought our equivocal common struggle, each of us had been huddled over their private desires, desires shaped by individual life stories full of un-pretty bits and nowhere near as noble as the revolutionary project had seemed to be at first sight. Sometimes malice was thrown into this mix, making it difficult to distinguish between private motivations and political ones. It was a type of malice that refused all kindness or mercy, an almost impersonal malice, closer to dogma but with a scorching force that always managed to find a new victim to consume and, so, survive.

All this had begun to bubble up to the surface even before 'the turn to pragmatism', when 'revolutionary action' started to become a disease-ridden swamp. Even back then, these types of militants were crazy about power—yes, power. They loved lording it over other people and sticking their noses into the way they chose to live their lives if at all possible. Grandstanding was their speciality. They constantly meted out carefully considered categorical judgements (the charge of 'bourgeois', for example, might be thrown at someone just because he or she was a cinema buff and was maybe even thinking about studying film). They were eager slaves to authority, in the role of master and servant both. They were the ones who exchanged revolution for money lust, the least ashamed of themselves of all their peers, and that's why they were the most successful at recycling their political past to secure lucrative positions in the new and savage world.

On the other hand, the great mass of followers of this exclusive petty-bourgeois elite were tossed into the grinder of daily subsistence, bled dry in the vicious whirlpool that is life in our country today, and isolated from one another, from public activism of any kind (which had more or less ceased to exist in any case) and from a past of which only the scars remained.

And because in these new times, possession and domination were the only things that mattered, the people who fell off the train found themselves with nothing to do but sink into depression. You can still find some of them hanging around the last of the cafes they used to frequent back in the day, practising the role of the disillusioned romantic who despises everything and everyone.

At the same time, a small minority was determined to continue the struggle. This group included two rare breeds of human being: the tragic-hero type, condemned to go on resisting hopeless collapse with great fortitude and self-abnegation, and the type that was the living ruin of an era dead and buried. This second type soldiered on, not out of solidarity with the people on whose behalf he supposedly struggled,[9] but because soldiering on is the destiny of the great. It wasn't a collective future that these types cared about; it was 'me', and 'my' contribution to 'the cause'. Isn't this precisely what Marxists call objectification? In any case, one can only imagine the levels of megalomania involved in such a situation. These people came to embody the corruption they had always believed to be somewhere 'out there'.

Now maybe the new favourite mantra of this elite of former militants makes more sense: 'self-realization'. When we were young, it used to mean the pursuit of a rich and full life beyond the imperative to accumulate money. Back then it was a way of being fully and

9 See 'ordinary people' in the dictionary of revolutionary intellectuals. We have in fact become so oblivious as to use this term shamelessly, and while it's true that 'ordinary' life is full of bland characters, so are the ranks of the left—none of them ever sprang from the head of a god.

practically in the world, of reaching into the creative and rebellious imagination to challenge the status quo and stir the waters of other people's lives. Today it means the hunt for a small spot under the sun, a foothold in the class pyramid that allows one to be conveniently oblivious to cunning and dishonesty—the mad pursuit of just one more privilege in the rush for privilege, to mount the top of the pile while denouncing it at the same time. This, then, is the ultimate luxury and these are the conditions in which they imagined—with astonishing naivety—they could create art. The very language they used to speak about creativity was the language of 'success and failure', fame and competition—the language of business, not the language of knowledge or beauty. Social distinction became a calling card for contracting friendships and inveigling invitations to 'progressive' galas. No wonder our generation only managed to produce mediocre talents.

Those who had prepared themselves to be heroes were nailed to the cross of their vanished ambitions. They had eagerly shouldered the burdens of the nation and launched the student movement with the noblest of intentions. They had come out from the confines of their narrow selves 'onto the wide street with its welcoming arms'.[10] They joined the people in their time of crisis and tried to create a future of their own

---

10 In the beautiful words of Salah Jahin.

making. On the street they discovered the heady taste of solidarity, the powerful clasp of living hands making a 'festival of the oppressed'. But when the festival was over, the 'struggle' turned into a desperate search for a way to fix their broken selves. Back then, we willingly offered ourselves as kindling for the struggle. Today the excuse for the existence of the struggle—any struggle—has become the need to assert a disarticulated selfhood. This is true, not just for the privileged few in their fashionable new circles but also for those engaged in 'serious' pursuits such as academic research and the highly sought-after graduate degrees that pave the way for jobs in prestigious international NGO networks. It's even true of those who carried on doing street-level organizing in working-class neighbourhoods. In all of this, the struggle became a mere accessory to our selves, a straw we clutched at in order to escape a world in which we too had become victims divided simply into rich and poor.

This portrait of the apostasy that swept through our generation isn't complete, however, without an account of love and marriage—the family.

One of the most significant differences between the seventies generation and the preceding one was that the former came of age in conjunction with a popular mass movement. It was a situation that pushed the seventies left to stay true to its principles, including in matters to do with sexual relations. The student movement drew many young women into mass politics, which was unprecedented in the history of the Egyptian left. Now for the first time, there was the possibility of moving beyond the schizophrenia that had historically defined the left's attitudes to women, including the particularly noxious ones of the sixties generation. They accepted the new ideas but continued to move and act in the totally conventional milieu of their upbringing. There was no radical questioning of sexual politics in their time. The Nasser regime made sedate calls for the integration of women into the workplace, but only in the context of its vision of the conventional family's social mobility—a vision in which women were enjoined to struggle alongside their husbands with the ultimate aim of rising into the ranks of the bourgeoisie. It was the only ambition that made sense. In this logic, a woman's social identity and status was defined according to her sexual function in relation to a man. She could only be an unmarried virgin, a wife, widow or divorcee (the lowest category). Otherwise she was simply a whore. All the talk about the right to work was just harmless, good-natured patter in the end—a pretty bauble that the virgin, wife, widow or divorcee could pin to her lapel. But woe to her if she stepped outside one of these roles! In the real world, the value of work and productivity were for men alone. The important point here is that these leftists processed their experiences with women, not through their 'principles' but through the psychology of the conservative milieu that shaped them. Their experience of love and sex was just a form of frivolous rebellion against entrenched social taboos rather than the much more difficult working-out of a set of new and freely chosen values. And so their experience—separate from and complicated by their principles—ended either in conventional marriage or in absurdly twisted and morally corrupt forms of sexual dissolution or simultaneously both.

The student-movement generation was the first generation of leftists that really believed in the dream of freely chosen relationships stripped of social calculation, relationships built on love and on non-coercive forms of commitment. It was a rosy dream and part of a much larger vision of changing the world, of inspiring and strengthening the bonds between lovers in ways that were bigger and more beautiful than each individual alone. Personal rebellion and political rebellion went hand in hand, were consistent with each other, drawing vigour and passion from the unencumbered years of youth.[11] Many young men married as a way to rebel against the wishes of their families. Marriage was the only socially acceptable form a relationship could take, after all. They married and, for a time, lived the fairy tale of impoverished domestic

---

11 The description isn't meant to be an absolute one, but this idea of love and relationship was a powerful current in the thinking of the generation as a whole.

bliss built on nothing but love and shared defiance. But it never took long for things to fall to pieces. Society was changing but not in the promised direction, and in spite of everyone's best intentions these relationships quickly acquired a conventional material basis. Some couples still held out for revolutionary transformation, but for most the real world imposed its laws, utterly transforming the space of love and marriage, its mechanisms and its place in their lives.

There was no longer a common dream, only a shared fear of the void, of economic insecurity and of the loneliness that afflicts a society in which people turn blindly inward, having once and for all lost the thread of the issues at stake—a society in which there is nothing to give and take but suspicion occasionally and utility, always, and in which thinking becomes a strange kind of vapid luxury. In such a society, people kill time with trivial amusements because they no longer believe they can be free.

In the middle of this general collapse, everybody began to search for some safe ground on which to land, and workplace and family became the primary refuge of the isolated and alienated individual. Former revolutionaries were no exception to this frantic search for a small private island of security; on the contrary, their need for it was even more pressing. The common ground that lovers had shared began to crumble under the weight of the real world and the authority of the family grew stronger. Then everything that was living and sincere in the relationship withered. Corporate conflicts between pairs of married couples began to emerge (so-and-so and his wife against so-and-so and his wife) while the couples themselves came apart at the seams.

The relationship falls back on dominant social norms and turns into an institution inside which husband and wife take shelter from the brutal world outside as well as from their private anxieties—anxieties constantly fuelled by feelings of impotence and self-deception, by the knowledge that the thing that unites them has nothing to do with what first brought them together. The evening parties of the chatterbox progressives that constitute their social lives only make matters worse. Neither partner is capable of offering the other support and human empathy in these pitiless conditions. Their stake in the institution is a selfish one and their illusions about each other are broken by the bald truth. At best they live in testy proximity because—in the bourgeois version of this marriage at least—expensive amusements aren't enough to paper over the fact that they are competitors. This new element is something that was absent in the 'traditional' family: competition, the need to assert oneself, to win something at the other's expense. The 'realism' of the sixties generation taught us something else too: infidelity was always and continues to be the main outlet for the inevitable conjugal boredom produced by the marriage institution and the thing that preserves the bourgeois family and its belongings intact. Today, opportunism is what unites husband and wife—their common interest that neither be cast out from a cruel multitude that tramples the uninvited. Having a family makes everything different; hence the obsession with property, with children and with maintaining a certain standard of living (so essential, and yet so costly) because the family must reproduce itself. The most important thing is getting up the ladder and staying there. This is how families disintegrate and become pitiful things. Why, after all, should they change, and to what?

Marriage becomes an impersonal affair. The person is only important insofar as they can play the role of husband or wife within the frame of the other's calculated self-interest. Marriage becomes an alienated relationship.[12]

This most private failure is part of the failure of a whole generation. In this place, the family—like all families in societies moving towards collapse— becomes nothing but a machine for domination ruled by the laws of private property and the struggle between spouses over mastery of the concern.

---

12 May I remind the reader that I speak here of a fairly common 'type'?

Between parentheses:

> The scions of the aristocracy are like beautiful, wilted plants in an abandoned garden. Some of them could have been counted among the most ethical intellectuals of this generation if the ferocity of the real world hadn't condemned them to eccentricity. Might it be a consolation to them that our entire society has become an absurdity?

3. *Two Examples*

> The petty bourgeois: when a person is incapable of understanding the world, he judges it.
>
> The haute bourgeois: the innocent egoist.

It's just not true that the bourgeois is 'uncomplicated' while the petty bourgeois is full of hang-ups. The hang-ups are different but they're there all the same. The life of the bourgeois is full of the most convoluted calculations—violence even, from childhood on. Unlike the petty bourgeois, these individuals never experience a period of 'innocence'. Their illusions about the world are shattered quite early on thanks to the infidelities of the father or the mother or both and to the social schemes and ambitions that the bourgeois family is forced to navigate in its daily life. It confidently teaches its children to boldly stare the world in the face, without ideological blinders or moral illusions of any kind. They learn right from the beginning that this world is made for the strongest—for them, for those who can seize it without moral qualms or 'high ideals'. These are props for the petty bourgeois alone. He needs them in order to face a world too vast and complex for him to understand, let alone see clearly, from the bottom of the social ladder where he stands. The game and all its players are only fully visible from the very top, after all. These props are the private chains of the petty bourgeois. They prevent him from seeing reality as it is. The more the pressure of this reality increases, the more he clings to his moral props, suffocating, while the abyss between the real world and what it should be continues to widen. His chains are both the consolation prize and the punishment for his social condition—physician and executioner, both. They engender that 'violence' that is particular to him, whether he suffers from the rancour of ambition or the struggle against it—it makes little difference. It is the violence of hatred, hatred of himself and hatred of the world that forces him to despair of ever being reconciled to it.

The life of the petty-bourgeois family becomes more brutal the lower down the social ladder one descends. But material want isn't the most pressing of its problems. There is something much more noxious: the struggle to survive in the whirl of the endless real and imaginary anxieties produced by the outside world. It strangles love and demands dogmatism, strict hierarchy and killing moral severity. When necessity rules the daily life of the petty-bourgeois family, the finer sentiments become luxuries that elicit contempt because they give the appearance of weakness. And the more this type of family is sealed off from the outside world, the more violent the shock of having to eventually confront that world. In this family, you learn fear before anything else, from the tyrannical father standing guard against the treacherous world outside. Prohibition always takes precedence over pleasure and satisfaction and shapes the rules of daily life, beginning with the most petty strictures—'Don't play in the parlour', 'Don't break your toys', 'Don't open the refrigerator without permission'—and inevitably ending with the most encompassing: 'Don't argue, obey in silence.'

In the father's world, the petty-bourgeois child is required to behave in an exemplary fashion, in other words, to act like a grown-up. The child never strikes out at this subjection of course. Instead, he swerves off into an interior world, a private corner that helps him to bear a reality in which he is nothing. In that little corner, he piles up his disappointments and his suppressed rancour and broods over it all with an intensity that borders on malice. He carefully hoards this secret bitterness; his reticence is as deep as his wounds, his pride in it as vast as his sense of humiliation. The world's indifference defeats him, and he learns that his feelings, his questioning, the torments that exhaust and drain him are unimportant, trivial even. An immense and unrealized life force is in this way transformed into a vast fund of destruction. This destructive energy normally never takes the form of barefaced power, for the petty bourgeois—and this we mustn't forget—is a 'moral' creature. The oppression he faces at the heart of his family is exercised in the name of morality and he in turn must have a moral excuse to unleash his bitterness onto the world. His childhood reticence turns into cowardice because he is unable to give true expression to a self disfigured by domination and coercion. He rarely dares to openly declare his hatred, for fear of poisoning his soul and damaging his social connections. Instead, he takes on the role of 'the martyr'; this is gratifying in a way that self-examination can never be. It soon becomes a need, a necessity. If excuses aren't available, he creates them. Usually, a woman provides this opportunity— his wife (the petty bourgeois doesn't normally have more than one). It doesn't matter whether she is the overbearing and 'quarrelsome' type or the 'kind and gentle' one: either way our constant victim succeeds in sucking her into his frustrated world. He imbues her with the same feelings of worthlessness that transform everything he touches. Instead of paying attention to her, he calls her insensitive and uncaring. She doesn't understand him or value him properly (according to his own opinion of himself, which is tailored to fit the length of his long persecution). She, like everything else, is a disappointment to him. In the end, his feelings towards her settle into silent contempt—which is exactly what he feels for himself. But in exceptional circumstances and if the opportunity arises, he takes the opposite tack. For example, if he acquires a position of authority, his other face immediately emerges; he becomes quite the despot. And if he can hitch his budding despotism to an ideological peg of some kind—'the cause' (or jihad)—it really takes wing. This is why it seems to me, at least, that no one is more dangerous than the educated, shy, honourable, moral-to-the-point-of-puritanism petty bourgeois, especially if he takes it upon himself to change 'the course of history'.[13]

The bourgeois also hates, and with no less violence than the petty bourgeois, but it is a polished, prudent and stealthy hate, with nothing of the other's bluntness and rancour.

Once he comes of age, the bourgeois who is raised to the idea that the world is his legitimate inheritance is obliged to discover the same truth as the petty bourgeois who has lost his innocence. That is, this world—this natural inheritance of his—turns according to the

13 This portrait is, of course, just an example of a type of the petit bourgeois that existed in the ranks of left militants in the 1970s. There may well be similar examples today, with the difference that now the petty-bourgeois family, while still conservative, believes in nothing.

rules of a savage game and that his inherited privileges are merely conveniences that do not exempt him from playing this game. So either he plays along with the necessary ruthlessness or he'll be torn to shreds by the gears of his paradise (for paradise has its victims too, even those to whom it is promised).

Since his parents have spared him the burden of learning how to calculate costs, he believes that the game is easy, honourable even, and that the mere fact of his presence at the top of the pyramid will take care of everything. This is how the petty bourgeois, bloated with envy, perceives him at least (and if he knew the truth, he'd lose his virginity a second time). The 'successful' petty bourgeois must lose his virginity. But there are also those who lose it and don't succeed, and these are the ugliest creatures to be found in a world created by the masters while the gods weren't looking.

The young bourgeois who shirks his responsibilities in the brutal game and relies on others to do all the work for him is ready prey for those who excel at adding and subtracting and who have practised playing the game long and hard in a trial of fire. They know that it never comes easy—even up there at the summit, especially there. The 'innocent egocentric' bourgeois must pay the price of the luxury—psychological above all else—that his parents surrounded him with. He was raised and fattened up only to be mounted by others! When this happens, the entire material and symbolic arsenal he has inherited cannot spare him the fate of the frail.

His difficult journey begins in the second half of life, much later than most people. It will never get any easier because he doesn't dare reject the rules of the game. He's incapable of pulling it all down. Even with the best of intentions, his flaccid muscles aren't up to the task. He's too accustomed to automatically getting the best out of every situation, never having to fight to the death for what he wants, never learning that every good thing has a price that must be paid sooner or later and that people of all classes—even the masters —pay this price with their living flesh. He just can't accept the fact that the same world that coddled and petted him is really a cruel place, even for the likes of him, the flower of his class. To change is difficult and exhausting: the world beyond his paradise is not a pleasant place. At least here there are plenty of pleasures and comforts that slow the haemorrhage of life and will, spirit and pride. He loses these things simply because he's lazy. He'd like to keep those soft pillows he once counted as the most trivial of accoutrements in a world that belonged to him and a mere taste of what was surely to come. Possessions now define his identity. He strains to forget the contradictions that tear his selfhood apart; the two poles of what was once a human being in the making. Pleasure and comfort are the coveted apples of bourgeois paradise as well as the banner of its decadence—the last signposts on the road taken by a class that lost its ability to dream, that has nothing to sell but pleasure.

The prostitutes they so despise are infinitely better than them. They at least aren't in the business of selling morals.

CHAPTER THREE
The Intellectual in Love

I love love and the whisper of love in glances
Love the smile, the tender tears of love
And the tremors that shake young breasts
Whether it's me who's loved or not.

Salah Jahin

When it comes to women, the intellectual takes his cue from the bourgeois. In other words, he plays the pimp. In thought and feeling though, he remains a petty bourgeois and hence deeply conservative. Armed with his cunning, he picks up the pieces of his erotic persona on his travels through class, a bag of tricks that includes the 'morals' of the 'lumpenproletariat'[1] (he doesn't understand that the absence of morals is not the same thing as nihilism). To make all this clearer, we have to go back to the bourgeois male, the model for our intellectual's unremittingly defensive conduct.

When the bourgeois male speaks of love, he really means an intense experience or 'state', the ephemeral heat that's inevitably followed by passion cooling and rational thinking kicking in. For him, love only exists

---

[1] Lumpenproletariat is the polite term for servants.

between these two poles. He knows from experience that the intensity will pass, like a sore throat, and leave not a trace but the inevitable price to be paid. The 'mature' ones refuse to believe in a thing called love; it's a mask people wear, a childish illusion, and when the illusion evaporates, all that's left is self-interest on the one hand and promiscuity on the other. The former leads to marriage and keeps it running smoothly; the latter does too. It compensates for the suffocating weight of a fictitious ideal of monogamy, and for the very real chains of property relations in bourgeois marriage. Property is the only truth in the world of the bourgeois, the fetish through which all roads cross.

A well-contracted marriage is part of the necessary, if unpleasant, order of things. So is debauchery, with no excuses made or lies told. Behind all the masks, this is the real stuff of bourgeois sexual relations—a terribly ugly thing, common and debased, with no pretty speeches or deceptive emotion or even the bare pretence of human kindness to dress it up.

It appears that the 'respectable' nature of sex in marriage doesn't satisfy the bourgeois male (though respectability in itself is of course de rigueur). And yet the bourgeois male is the fiercest champion of monogamy in marriage—and with good reason too, for he must be sure of his heirs after all. Whoring is the only real alternative to the castrated pleasures of marriage (though 'whoring' is usually what women do; men 'conquer'). Whoring is the bourgeois male's practice of the thing he names 'freedom' (much like his petty-bourgeois brother), an oddly neutered kind of whoring, because it is a form of theft.

But there are also other, more significant dynamics at work. When the last waves of rapture ebb and our man raises his head like a ball bobbing on the surface of the water, he discovers that he hasn't drowned in love after all; his habitual waxen and calculating expression is still there. The erotic experience is his private little fortress of freedom, built on the mutually agreed exploitation between man and woman, a dependable relation that takes a variety of complex and well-established forms. For example, he provides financial support and she provides pleasure and distraction. She is like a court jester. It's her job to entertain him, to provide relief from a long and profitable day's work. Now he naturally wants to spend money and amuse himself. She goes along with this, and how much he spends will be determined by the degree of her social value and utility. On the other hand, the respectable woman marries a respectable man so as to take possession of him and his amenities. If marriage is out of the question, she'll have an affair with him. Or she'll have an affair out of marital boredom. She longs for love, so she goes looking for it. She's used to the idea that her femininity has an exchange value. The mere fact of being a woman gives her the right to a price, and it's doubtful whether she's ever asked herself why this should be so. Love doesn't come cheap after all, and poverty is the parent of revolution and crime. No matter how 'refined' the couple's relationship may appear, their prison lies between these two poles. The power of their bourgeois laws is beyond even them and anyone who forgets this is likely to meet a sorry fate. Bourgeois justice does not protect the gullible.

The only freedom exercised here is the freedom to choose the 'product', and the 'customer'. In a relationship where sex is a commodity, there is no room for love; the relationship between buyers and sellers is one of conflict—fraud, if possible. When the laws of property that rule the bourgeois couple and foreclose the possibility of love crumble, the laws of the market step in to take their place. It all comes to the same thing in the end: marriage or prostitution.

1. *The End of Bourgeois Love Is Death*

And sex is never gratifying. Money can't breathe life into dull pleasures, and so the cycle repeats itself and the affliction becomes the remedy. Incontinence, promiscuity, perversion—nothing can cure the bourgeois male's infatuation with sex, which incidentally exists in inverse proportion to his ability to enjoy it.

Youth passes, dreams turn to illusion and love becomes mere sexual appetite, ennui held at bay. It is a nightmare landscape devoid of human beings, of human expression, and where the only sound to be heard, in the words of the poet Salah Abd al-Sabbur, is the sinister beat of 'the thumping of a woman's thigh between a man's buttocks'.[2]

They say that in African tribal societies, when a hunter killed an animal, he took possession of its powers and thereby acquired great strength. The same is true of bourgeois love. It is an act of hunting, of mastery and submission and, finally, of killing.

But when you kill a human being, you don't acquire new powers. There is just a void left behind. A part of your deepest self collapses (that self that is so dear to the bourgeois male, so exquisite in its uniqueness). The one condition of the successful hunt is that your eyes should never meet those of the dying animal. If they do, you'll be cursed by its anguished, accusing gaze. But you're really just fooling yourself. Curse or no curse, retribution is always prompt. The destiny of lovers is shaped in the heat of the struggle between hunter and prey.

For the bourgeois, all roads lead back to the sovereign self and the constant struggle to assert this self at the expense of other selves. The highest purpose

---

2 [From the poem 'The Shadow and the Cross' published in the 1961 collection *Aqulu lakum* (*I Say to You*).]

of life is unencumbered pleasure, stripped of the burden of giving and taking. The world of the bourgeois is shaped by this aspiration, in love (the sense, the means, the ends) as in much else.

It always begins with pleasure. But the bourgeois lover only wants pleasure for himself. Where are the limits and what of the other person? The problems begin when things start to get serious. But why should they get serious in the first place? This is love after all, not marriage! It's quite possible to squeeze out some pleasure from the space that precedes serious intimacy. In this space, there is no real knowledge of the other person. Love is a game or a form of masturbation. The love object is beside the point. The point is the drunken 'state' itself, the 'arousal' that the other can excite in him, a set of 'tactics' skilfully managed: seduction, bullying, brinksmanship and the carrot of conciliation at just the right time. Timing here is important, and detail, as they are in any polished game. The raw intimacy of sex plays no role in bringing the lovers closer together. Instead, it becomes a way to take advantage of the other's weakness in order to control them. Weakness in the bourgeois creed is not a human frailty but an unpardonable defect. Deepening knowledge of the other is no longer an avenue to love as it was before the emergence of the bourgeois life-worlds that rule us. It produces alienation instead. The stronger party must remain a mystery to the other, must prevent them from acquiring the keys to their psyche. The stronger party's ability to manoeuvre lies precisely in this obscure space. If the other manages to take hold of it, the space will disintegrate. Once transparency and vulnerability are allowed in, the power to manipulate is lost, boredom sets in, and the relationship loses all meaning. This is why in both love and marriage, keeping up appearances—and hiding the truth—is of cardinal importance to the game. Knowledge is not a means to intimacy but a means to possession and power; and for the bourgeois, that which can be possessed loses its value. It becomes a mere acquisition, unloved and neglected by an owner who hasn't wasted any energy in getting it, a thing for consumption only.[3] The lover is the one who has not yet been mastered and possessed, and the condition of love is the period of struggle over the keys to power—that stretch of time when the roles of conqueror and conquered have not yet been determined and where the point of climax is the beginning of the countdown.

The conclusion of intimacy requires an act of killing. Love would die on its own in any case if it weren't for the craving to milk some last drops of titillation from the finished affair, a mopping-up operation that becomes a form of torture. The game of

---

3 This is a description of love and not marriage, where acquisition is the supreme value. There can be no idle talk of love in marriage.

mastery played by this extreme version of the practised seducer ends in bloodlust and in real hatred for his prey. He can only truly be captured by a person who is capable of annihilating him. His contempt for people in general is nurtured by his unending contempt for the opposite sex, and he finally arrives at a point where the only people he can respect are the ones who can make him feel like the insect he is. Only then will he be convinced that this person truly knows him.

This is why love doesn't offer any kind of real human experience to bourgeois lovers—the human is always placed at a safe distance to begin with. Neither does it provide the 'novelty' that each of the parties so desperately seeks because they can only renew their pleasure by repeating the game. But sometimes fortune frowns on our bourgeois friend; he is captured and he falls in love, and now it's his turn to play the role of prey. (How easy it is to be free of 'illusions' about love when you turn it into a trivial, twisted game.) His understanding of love never rises above that of an adolescent. He'll never grow into an emotionally mature adult because it demands the single most diffi-cult condition for him to fulfil: to give as well as to take.

One of two fates awaits the bourgeois once he's 'freed of illusions'. He becomes an expert at the game. A dark emptiness spreads and deepens inside him. Now our friend slips into sadomasochism, a kind of final surrender to emotional death. This is not 'nihilism'. It's the deliberate practice of inflicting pain.

A person who is empty of emotion is a force of violence and hatred. Cruelty is the mechanism that compensates for his frustration. He's given up on intimacy, and so he digs deeper and deeper into his wound with compulsive pleasure. His sadomasochism cannot compensate for the fulfilment that it sends into permanent exile. It turns its victims into onanists, utterly helpless in the face of the real thing. The more he embraces his impotence, the more his cruelty grows, and he finds artful ways to perfect it to compensate for the deadening boredom of repetition.

Or he is prudent and pragmatic and he marries (not for love of course; how silly that would be). In the game, the marriage option is serious business. Because marriage is built out of the most basic laws of bourgeois social relations, the husband can only be one of two things: master or slave. Bourgeois 'rights and duties' don't change this reality one bit. Self-interest structures the hierarchy of rights and duties in bourgeois social relations and produces the real, hidden logic of relationships between people, even in love and marriage.

For the bourgeois, life is a battle for survival of the fittest (a lesson it teaches in turn to the petty bourgeois). The price of this conviction is steep; he pays it from the deepest part of his private life. The primitive hunter killed with respect and awe. The bourgeoisie trampled the person, closed the circle and impaled itself on its own sword.

In bourgeois society, our lives—our most private relationships—have become a form of organized slavery. Love will always be a pretty dream until we put an end to possession and the logic of cowardice and coercion in relationships, relationships that would surely die if they ever breathed the air of freedom. Love is only possible as the exercise of free will between free individuals. The 'realists' will laugh and wink but the contemptible truth of love and marriage in our society gives us no choice but to dream.

2. *An Interlude on Innocence*

In the spectacle of the (Egyptian) intellectual's relations with women, ghosts from another time and place haunt the living. Though money and social capital are absent from the intellectual's theatre of action, exploitation is still the name of the game. The bourgeois logic of buying and selling (capitalism), which is at least governed by laws, turns into a game with no rules, a game in which everything is allowed and winner takes all, a con man's game actually (and a secondary symptom of capitalism).

The young woman who accepts a date with an intellectual doesn't dare hope for a fancy outing, or even a not-so-fancy one. You'll find her heading for a decrepit cafe where her young intellectual will buy her a glass of bitter boiled tea and sell her a bunch of 'progressive' dreams that cost him nothing but a string of his cheapest merchandise: talk. Talk about 'justice' that he himself is no longer quite sure he believes in; the kind of talk that a sheltered and oppressed petty-bourgeois girl desperately longs to hear. Or she might be an upper-middle-class girl looking for a bit of danger (all the better for him as she's sure to taste of the considerable cost that went into her upbringing).

And so our young man talks about justice, and the hypocrisy of social values, and a lot of other things besides. But the most important thing—the real purpose of it all—is the talk of 'free love'—love liberated of money and of responsibility of any sort, love raised on 'personal responsibility' with no social consequences whatsoever. Our intrepid intellectual plunges into this particular theme with a persistence that he sometimes lacks in other, no less momentous matters. Of course his 'personal responsibility' is to be borne by one party alone. It's a fairy tale in a society built on relentless interference in the private lives of individuals (marriage and divorce, personal-status laws, etc.). The truth is that there is only *social* responsibility and society always calls to account those who sign on the state's dotted line.[4] Otherwise, personal responsibility is just a favourite subject of private and often

---

4 [Salih is referring to the way in which the state mediates normative social domination of private relationships in the form of legislation and penalty.]

malicious gossip about such-and-such couple. The gatherings at which this gossip transpires represent society's moral authority, and so of course they judge (i.e. condemn) one party alone: the woman, the party who is always magically transformed by all the talk about 'personal responsibility' into a whore (our Arab intellectuals excel at this type of miraculous trans-mutation). As for the man, his personal responsi-bility becomes an affirmation of his virility, and he struts and preens for all comers (literally and not jokingly). There was, in what we call our 'backward' values, a finer conception of manhood, one that was based in a rich legacy of ethical striving. Our genera-tion simply dropped the nobility of the ideal and kept the backwardness.

And so free love ends up being free-ride love. But what of it? Just another idea in the archive of grand and inspiring ideas that become clichés in the cafes of the Egyptian intellectual. This one is neither more nor less noble than any of the other ones they've cheap-ened. Whether they like to admit it or not, it's one of the cornerstones of their vast hollowness. Death does not spare this most intimate and private part of them, the core of human identity. And yet how proud they are of their 'realism'!

Being a man, the intellectual requires innocence in a woman. But innocence that doesn't allow for any kind of comprehension of the ways of the world isn't much more than a form of idiocy (and in this the 'not-innocent' woman has the advantage). Our friend considers it his right to exploit her. His logic is that since she's accepted exploitation, she deserves it. Her innocence—as experience always shows him—is a fragile thing. And there's more. If this fool can't himself understand the 'complexity' of his precious soul, how can he possibly hand it over to her, the stupid one? She must be content with his precious body. If he's a determined reformed romantic, he'll be sure to set her straight.

There is a secondary issue here, nonetheless an important one. Washed-out intellectuals adore smashing idols of every kind: creativity, success, fame. They love it so much that not being able to do some smashing slays them with frustration. Proving that 'everything is false and worthless' is an endless need for them; they are like punctured water-skins that must haemorrhage water. This is also how they judge women (they know them inside out, of course). Women are only good for one of two things: either to be a stupid wife (not worthy of her man) or a crafty slut (not worthy of her man either). Any other 'type' of woman is a mythical creature. A completely unsurprising paradox follows. When the Egyptian intellectual fantasizes about 'woman', he is an incurable romantic. The creature of his imagination is the little goddess of literary endeavour, healing all wounds and compensating for all losses and betrayals (and there are many indeed). She embraces and enfolds, she offers the comfort and security that is to be found in her arms alone. On top of this, she is—of course— very beautiful. Her eyes are black or hazel or green but they are always wide. She has perfect breasts imported from Europe, firm and round and supple; they bounce up and down like rubber balls (the favoured description of novelists). Of course this exalted goddess is not one iota more of a real person than the slut or the clumsy wife. She too lives in a notional prison that endlessly reproduces the triangle of goddess, wife and whore. She is forced to conform to his taxonomy whether she likes it or not. Between the coarseness of the reality and the fantasy, experience can build no bridges. It can never be enriching, because instead of being something that connects two people to each other in a continuous dialogue, it's a one-way street inside one person's head, his head; a street that's blocked between cruel ideation on one end, and fantasies of escape and transgression on the other.

For the intellectual, a woman's 'morals' are synonymous with her sexual behaviour. She might well be a predatory beast—society will neither object to this nor punish her for it. In fact, this is exactly the horrible revenge that women often take on men in general. She fulfils his expectations of her: she makes him her prey. She's definitely not a 'rebel', she's a pragmatist, exactly like him. Society itself teaches women how to circumvent its morals—morals that are precise and consistent and logical because we drink them with our mother's milk. This is how duplicity becomes 'logical' and 'natural'. Oppression teaches her to be cunning and humiliation teaches her malice and hate. It's her arsenal in the battle for 'survival of the smartest', which is the real battle being waged in the real world (not some silly struggle between vice and virtue). And so she's treated by society (and by men in particular) like a despicable creature, incapable of nobility. She's taught to debase herself and she learns to despise weakness and modesty and sincerity, and to admire aggressiveness and vulgarity and power. She learns how to see men as prey, how to turn them into prey, because this is the real 'social contract', the law of the world she lives in.

(And slaves continue to reproduce slaves—people who are incapable of facing the world naked of everything but their freedom to choose. Their legacy is a poison, a manufactured epidemic.)

When this finishing school for girls is run by intellectuals, you'll find the most dangerous type of woman of all. T. S. Eliot once wrote something to the effect that women invest in their upper regions so as to double the value of their nether parts. These are women who surely learnt about life in our finishing school. They're really good at holding forth on 'pressing' social issues with their sights set much further down. And yet our society demands that women alone blush with shame.

Personal Documents

DOCUMENT 1

Cairo, 15 December 1988

My dear [. . .]

I'm writing to you without being quite sure I'm going to finish this letter because I don't know that I'm really up to it. The idea of writing about myself, for myself, seems too obscene, though for over a year now I've been feeling that I really have to go over my accounts. It's such an unsavoury business, first of all because I learnt this game of self-examination early on from the intellectuals, then during my time of political activism it became a kind of repulsive secret habit, or an impossible indulgence, like the play of a child who still thinks it's the centre of the universe. The other reasons are all more or less related. It was my slowly coming to terms with the real world, etc., that eventually healed me, not this type of navel-gazing.

Maybe getting fired from my job finally forced me to confront a decisive period in my life: what my political work really meant to me as well as the heartache I've been going through for the past year. Now there's some time to confront all that head on, the demons that I let sleep while I tried to discover the world without fear. I believe I've managed to conquer a sizeable chunk of those demons in an obscure kind of way, but I can't venture to say with any boldness how many are left to deal with, and what they look like. I must have an accounting! Not so I can 'grow up' (perfection is for God alone!) but because I need to find a road to walk that I can be sure of. I've had enough of aimlessness, of letting life take me by the hand and lead me along.

Or the real problem is that I lack the emotional energy one needs to write. When you write with deep feeling, flashes of extraordinary insight tend to overwhelm abstract thinking. Everyone has this ability to capture epiphany; they just have to seize it from the stream of reflection. In moments like that you stop thinking—you don't have time to think, even about the way you express yourself in words overflowing the page, lit up by the living truth like jewels. Truth you never knew until it crystallizes in front of you like a prophecy.

During the short time that my feelings for [. . .] grew, feelings I had to murder in cold blood, the tenderness that suddenly spilt out from that land of the dead inside me opened up doors of discovery and marvellous visions. At times like that, you become pellucid with concentrated sight in the parched darkness. Your mind lights up with understanding. And yet in the middle of all that glory, I couldn't see the horrible torment that [. . .] was going through. I often wonder how Dostoevsky managed to see both the gentleness and the cruelty in people. That's a tough one, my brother, and just maybe it's the reason I'll never make a good writer. (Now don't you dare believe me, it's just a little joke to lighten the melodrama!).

You know, during the last battle at work, it really hit me how much that type of fight beats down your humanity, and I couldn't stop thinking about our political days. But I don't quite understand why the conflict over posts and positions, etc., is so ruinous (to my mind, objectification isn't a good enough explanation, but what the hell . . .). My nemesis in that battle was a class apart in the category of dirty scoundrels, a twisted individual with no bottom lines. He knew his mask of rectitude was shattered and that he could never fix it. The special mark of this type of person is that they've lost the ability to feel shame. When the right moment comes, they'll slit your throat without a second thought. Their cruelty is like a darkness that obscures their faces. You struggle to make out their features but all you can see is terrifying emptiness. This rare type of individual makes up one out of ten dirty scoundrels at the most. I've rarely ever encountered them, except in Dostoevsky's fiction. But there's always something in them that defies my understanding, a possibility or potential, and I find myself wondering what that potential might have looked like if it wasn't devoted to utter venality.

To move on though (!): The dramatic ending to the experiment that I pointedly and smugly presented to my 'comrades' as the 'life force' that saved me from the fate of 'death by drowning'[1] in my sharp (and regretted) book brought me face to face with an urgent question. To what extent was I just trying to escape my own estrangement from this life? Secondly—and this is the uncomfortable, and also somewhat frightening question to my mind—to what extent had I overcome my old troubles? To what extent had I solved the puzzle that had cost so many before me their heads? How did the fine dream stumble and fall in the land of diseased realists? I have to admit, the harm they did me still hurts much more than the memory of any goodness on their part. But another way of putting the question (far from any poetic considerations) would be to ask: Did I manage, after this long and difficult journey, to become someone capable of dealing with the real world without losing either her balance or her dreams?

It's in this sense that I go back again (or maybe it's the fifth or sixth time already) to the beginning, in an attempt to answer questions I imagined I had solved. But then I think about your quite sound objections to the concept of 'the people' as an ontological expression. What does 'life' mean, or 'dream' for that matter? What is 'balance'? Passing time makes all the

---

1 The title of a novel by Abd al-Hakim Qasim [1934–90].

difference when it comes to what words like these mean, the questions they open up. I know this is true for my own experience.

Maybe it's time to stand up and ask myself in all honesty what exactly I was looking for when I became a communist. What did communism mean to me exactly? The question seems trivial and senseless to anyone who's freely chosen the life of a militant. For someone like me, it's a dangerous question. I had always considered my relationship to communism as a given even though I suspect that, deep down, the question was always there (without the same depth and clarity as now) and I did try to give an answer once in a letter to a friend. What I said then was that communism gave order and intelligibility to a world that never appeared to me to be just or logical, a place of boundless suffering. Maybe my problem with politics was finally nothing more than my problem dealing with everyday life in the real world. Don't I remind you of a brave and noble Don Quixote type falling victim to a low trick? In my case it was a despicable, if hilarious, political farce that laid me low.

All through my life—a long one by now—the thing that always protected me and kept me from falling down was a faith that bound me to other people (though I'm actually quite terrified of them in daily life). It was a faith rooted in my deep feeling for the magnificence of human achievement. When I was an adolescent, it was Dostoevsky who first helped me to understand that my suffering was both comprehensible and justified. It was a child's first deed of affiliation —a child frightened by something in the vast ocean that we call the world. In Dostoevsky, even the contemptible is beautiful (thanks to the genius of the human heart). But there was no one to tell me at the right time that heads will roll in that space between the luminous beauty of the work of art and the real world that it portrays.

It might be that my personal destiny first began to unfold in that distant moment, that my truest bond to the real world began as hard faith in the great art created by people striving to discover their dream and to make it real, to keep it pure and shining, innocent of their own corruption. But in all my direct, unmediated relationships with these same people, I was incapable of truly understanding them or even interacting with them. I lacked the simplest bonds of trust to bind me to them. It was as though the real world was determined to mock my well-fortified faith, that private citadel I took shelter in from reality's sharp teeth. I don't think I can hide any more. The real world has pronounced its judgement (it always gets the last word it seems). I haven't been able to read much of anything for a whole year now. My thirsting to learn and understand is still there but I can no longer find the peace I used to get from books. I just don't know. Is it because living inside your mind all the time turns you into an aging and detached observer? Or is it just the solitude —the long absence of the human warmth that can give you strength to endure the trials of the journey? That warmth is all dried up in me now; it can't sustain itself on yesterday's crumbs and broken illusions. And yet every time I picked myself up off the ground and soldiered on, I was recreating the same illusion! I used to tell myself that I'd merely taken a wrong turn, that I'd keep on searching, but the same old fantasy about the beauty in 'people' (certainly not the ones I actually knew) always dragged me down again. Now, in the end, when I look inside me, I find nothing but a mass grave.

I wonder if this is the secret behind my chronic and deeply buried feeling of ineptitude: inadequacy in the face of political action and cowardice in the face of writing (and even teaching). Now it's taken over my old love of books, my one sure stronghold. Maybe this is just the story of a girl who was never taught how to be brave. But I did learn an eloquent and expensive lesson in fact: that strength and weakness are a journey, not some kind of gift or personal destiny. I know that there is something in the story of my monumental breakdown that's deeply real, and also a daring that those who kept going can never understand. I refused to patch up my holes with rags—with a family, a child, or even with the dogged resistance to facing the world

naked, with no fig leaves, not even the fig leaf of political struggle. Drowning men clutch at straws. There
are people of whom nothing is left once you've sub-
tracted the militant. That's because their relationship
to the human beings on whose behalf they fight is cor-
rupted, and so their 'struggle' falls to pieces in spite
of their sincerity. I've seen people who kept on going
despite having hardly any real contact with flesh-and-
blood human beings. For them, the struggle is a form
of condescension.

In the past few years, during the period when I
abandoned politics and tried to throw myself into the
arms of 'ordinary people', I liked to imagine myself as
part of a huge human procession stretching back into
history, encompassing all the legions united by a
common dream that no individual or party can possibly monopolize. That's why I felt I was still a communist by right, even though I was no longer a militant;
it was my right to pronounce on positions and tactics.
But now I know better. To go on making such claims
would constitute a form of (well-intentioned) fraud.

You know, these past months, I've been reading a
bit about the Chinese C[ommunist] P[arty] and buying
everything I could find by Hegel, but realized that I'd
been avoiding anything about Palestine and the
Intifada.[2] It's a serious lapse that I can't deny to be

---

2 [Salih wrote this letter during the first Palestinian intifada of
1987–93.]

sure. But this isn't what concerns me now. What I'm really struggling to understand is the basis of my relationship to this life. What is it that truly connects me to other people? 'Knowledge' isn't enough here; action—the space of action—is everything. I suspect that my death lurks in some corner of that space. But all the talk about escapism aside, you can never truly *understand* without *doing* (of this you see, experience makes me sure), without dirtying your hands in the everyday, without discovering its categorical meaning, because without this meaning, life becomes an equivocal and therefore a fragile and tenuous thing.[3]

I also suspect that there's a strong connection between my fear of facing 'the real world', that puritanical honesty of mine that people so admire, and the strange balance of strength and weakness in my character. The honesty is a damned problem. It certainly isn't as pretty as it seems at first glance. It's passed irrevocable death sentences on so many people I've encountered in my life. I couldn't understand them and therefore I was afraid of them. It's also why I was afraid of life, even as abstract idea. It was like living in a fairy tale. There are the villains who have to pay in the end, and there are the good characters with whom I identified, of course, until they showed their other scoundrel face—at which point I would fall back in

---

3 This path to this discovery is much more difficult than most Marxist parrots can imagine.

horror. My fear of others was always accompanied by an overwhelming desire to surrender myself completely. This is why I was never able to understand them. And this is why it was always me who got hurt. The death sentences were deserved to the degree that I believed in the power of the condemned over me. I demanded of others exactly those things that I lacked; they were a bolster to prop up my cracked self. I begged all newcomers to heal me of past betrayals, and through it all, my 'puritanical honesty' left me wide open—it was really a cry for help. I never even noticed that those other people were also wounded and incomplete, just like me. Besides, to me, people were just an abstract noun: 'the human being', so beautiful and perfect. I myself was not such a creature, I knew that, of course. But I could neither understand nor forgive the fact that they weren't either.

Only now do I really understand why I felt such humiliation during the time I was ill. It had slowly accumulated with every slap given when I reached out my hand to another human being. I only wanted to hear the magic words that would finally give me some peace. It amazes me now, how I managed to hold on to my pride both before the illness and after it, how I managed not to despise it—life's ironical little joke on gullible me. 'The immortal petty bourgeois,' as the poet said, 'is a bundle of contradictions.'

Have I confused you with all this jumping around between communism and stargazing, puritanism and weakness, etc.? But I want you to help me understand the quixotic elements of this story. As I said right at the beginning, my relationship to communism and my relationship to life are one and the same thing, and both equally problematic. Well, now that we've gone this deep, maybe it's the right time to come back up to the surface. Let's take the obvious route back, the place where we ended, so that we can answer the questions we left unanswered. I'll try to be brief because we're really almost finished now.

Let's go back to the triangle of fear, honesty and strength/weakness from a slightly different angle. You all demand that I write, and you say that I have the necessary imagination and honesty to do it. It reminds me of something Ernst Fischer wrote in his marvellous book *The Necessity of Art*. He says that art is like a thoroughbred mare: it will humiliate the mediocre writer, but the true artist knows how to tame and master it. At this point, and for the record, I want to state my doubts about my mastery of language. Art (writing in this case) isn't just mastery of an instrument but an inspired vision of the real. We celebrate art as 'creation', the creation of an absolute, of the dream, from the heart of the ordinary, and even of the commonplace. In order to make the dream shine with brilliance, it must be watered with that immortal thing that endures at the core of the humble, transient moment (and the truth of which never occurs to 'ordinary people'). But who among us has this awe-some ability? I suspect my little joke at the beginning of this letter hit the mark after all! You'd have to be ter-ribly bold to stretch wide open and really take in the common source of all this brutality and sweetness. You'd have to discover the humanity in meanness and venality so as not to be just another petty-bourgeois moralist, let alone an artist.

You're all asking me to show a kind of courage and ability that I just don't have. Writing requires a rich sensibility. Where could I possibly have acquired such a thing? From the narrative of my scars? Fear is a dull and plodding thing. You once said that I was 'a hero of our time in shades of grey'. So to be fair to myself, I'll make a list of those periods when I did manage to write. It's a short list to be sure, but maybe that's because the times in question were so electric and bursting with life.

1. My diaries, written between the ages of 16 and 18. This was the '68 moment, a time of enor-mously productive turmoil and soul-searching, aborted, in your correct opinion, in the wake of the 1973 war.

2. Political writings, from 1972–73. This was the moment when we finally seemed to have found our way, me included, but it turned out that we were really in the process of giving up the ghost.

3. Finally, the book I wrote abroad. I had managed to get away from the story of my long
   and obscene journey in the world of politics.
   Luckily for me, I landed in a place of undam-
   aged beauty, with no burdens to carry, with no
   customary price to pay, no shattered illusions
   to mourn. But it turned out there was a price
   to be paid, after all. I was so very tired. I was
   the casualty of my own escape from a life
   weighed down by thinking beyond my abilities, condemned to sterility because I was a
   prisoner of fear. I couldn't breathe. I made a
   leap of faith into life, and so it was inevitable
   that I lost my balance. It subsequently occurred
   to me—as was also inevitable —that I bore the
   past a grudge and that that was why I wrote a
   highly poetic and poisonous book. There was
   no escaping the noxious fumes of the past.
   Now I'm certain that it was the last stages of
   writing that book that brought on the schizophrenia (forgive me if I digress here, but the
   issue continues to dog me).

The vision of that beauty—so distant from my
depressing reality—was my passion, and also my
undoing. Might I reach for it all over again, even
though now I know better? I know that I'm passing
final sentence, not just on my relationship to communism (to which I'm still deeply attached, if only in the

most abstract sense) but also on my relationship to writing, and to those few individuals who keep me anchored in the world. I'm passing final judgement on myself, and while I'm just barely getting to know the world around me no less. I'm so late to this place and yet here I am trying to begin all over again at a time when there's nothing left to be discovered. There's no more wall of beauty for me to hide behind, even if I'm prepared to pay the price of hiding. But the real question is: Would I still have the wherewithal to pay after all this time?

Salah Jahin was right when he said that 'you're a fool if you fear the promise', but the other true thing he didn't say and didn't need to say is that the grand finale isn't always a happy one: 'Reached it or not, what do I really care / And why . . . The pleasure was in the love affair!' Honestly, I never for a moment regretted taking the only possible path to rediscovering the world. But the things that happened to me during the trip were beyond my endurance, because I had to bear them alone above all. All the world's sweetest dreams combined can't compensate for a single moment of warmth expressed in a human face. It was an over-whelming desire for some kind of human connection that drew me on and gave me courage on the journey —so you can imagine how heavy the burden of defeat was. I really tried to go on, and that, in spite of con-stantly colliding with the brutal laws governing the relationships between intellectuals ruled in turn by an even more brutal reality. I include in this description both the old generation ('the prodigal sons' come back to the lap of the regime) and the new generation, beaten down before they even got the chance to make their share of history. By the time I turned to 'ordinary people', the ugliness was everywhere. So my question to you is: Where do I begin? There's no shelter for my own dreams in this world. But what do I care! I'm incapable of living in it, let alone writing about it. I only want to hold on to the dream in the teeth of my febrile imagination, and my so-called honesty. It's no coincidence that I was never able to write anything but diaries and pseudo-memoirs except during a brief and fortuitous period. In the same way, the student movement was a moment that shone out briefly in the era of the bourgeoisie, before its dark age had descended. The limits of my imagination are the limits of my courage to act, and those times when I was brave enough to let it soar marked the points in my life when I was most disconnected from reality. This is not the imagination that creates art—art that 'knows' reality and that is born of this knowledge, not of the escape from it. The 'honesty' of this type of imagination remains hostage to reality. It's the honesty of someone who is incapable of discerning her dreams in the outlines of other people's faces (my passionate defence of 'ordinary people' notwithstanding). Maybe this isn't my fault alone but the fault of the times I've lived through and the people I've known in them. But it's my own, real experience and I'm compelled to admit in the end that I keep colliding with that ever-widening abyss between what is and what should be. Now I understand that the real world is drawn in shades of grey that tend to annihilate dreams and dreamers together. My imagination was too sickened to survive. I couldn't find a foothold in this world or bring a new one into being. But this personal seeking be damned, the real question is how to find a way out of the miserable state of affairs engulfing Egypt and its people. My honesty still gives me a great deal of freedom to choose my position without embarrassment, but it's clear now that this freedom is the product of the vast distance that separates my dreams from reality, including the reality of my country. All I can do now is escape to a place where none of this violence and brutality exists, a place where I don't have to be ashamed of having fled.

Believe me, I never imagined at the beginning of this inquest that the results would be so grim to make me almost regret having started out in the first place. I suppose that's what most of the men and women of my generation came to. But I really did believe that I'd made some headway in achieving a measure of emotional balance—in establishing a real foundation for my relationship to the world around me. It seemed like a big achievement to me, especially since I'd done it without the protection of the institutions that most of my generation took refuge in. I was a vagabond, with no social position of any kind, no fixed residence —a guest at my sister's house. Imagine then that the only real value of this achievement turned out to be the certainty that I'm sentenced to exist on the margins of life because I'm just not up to its battles.

I was fired from my job because of my contempt for the rules; at the same time my proud little self has no means of defence against these same rules. This is the law everywhere. Do you think that writing requires a little less self-flagellation? Doesn't any kind of work entail some kind of conflict with colleagues? In my political life I ran like hell from conflict but it was always imposed on me in spite of anything I might want, everything I tried to do to avoid it. They would not let me observe them from my lofty perch. It was never about money or jockeying for position, they just wanted to smash my arrogance.

And now what? What am I to do? I find myself in a completely unexpected bind. Does the idea of escaping abroad really mean early retirement from life? On the other hand, I'm too exhausted to keep wringing my own neck. The only way I can stay in Egypt is to do something that will give me some kind of renewed faith and inner peace; otherwise I've got to go, no matter the price. (Please note that I haven't said one word about how as a single woman, I'm surrounded by a vicious pack of wolves—a very important footnote to my current position.) I wonder if there are some opportunities here that I'm wasting by contemplating leaving. Or am I really and truly all used up by now?

It's really painful to find myself face to face with the same confounded question that tormented me during my illness. What can I do? I thought I'd flung it aside once and for all in a passion of fury. All that new-fangled chatter about 'self-realization' is just a way of saving your own hide from the sinking ship. It's all about looking for excuses to justify and inflate your own existence while the people around you are being crushed en masse: you must, above all, avoid the fate of those 'others', must never share in the profound tragedy of their collective fate. In the context of this tragedy, the endless quest for self-realization smacks of alienation from the get go, of something inhuman, because 'people' and their problems, and any kind of pressing debates and struggles—in politics or in art— are transformed into mere 'instruments' for proving oneself, for raising oneself above the 'level' of ordinary people (no two intellectuals would disagree over the truth of this but it's rare to find a single one of them acting differently). I truly hated this way of seeing the world and I still do. I hate how that thing we call 'self-realization' has become a kind of badge of qualification for any human connection. Without it you tumble down into the ranks of those decidedly uninteresting 'ordinary people'. There's a whiff of fascism about this attitude.

You know, all your ideas about the importance of the 'historic project' offer a really important insight into all this. It's true that since the beginning of the bourgeois revolutions, intellectuals inspired by grand projects saw themselves as being part of a movement much bigger than the small space of the individual. Believing that their struggle was relevant to all the people, that their role in it was 'for the people' was what set fire to their imagination and their passion. The declension of Egyptian intellectuals into isolated individuals trying to save themselves from the flood is part of the entire people's loss of their collective hopes—their decomposition into isolated units connected by nothing but the struggle for survival, and we all pay the price. It's clear that real creativity is deeply connected to grand projects and that consequently our intellectuals, by themselves, are unlikely to produce anything but mediocrity. It's the people who first have to see their way clear to any such project, not the vanguard. The whole question of revolution has become so immensely complicated after all the defeats suffered at the hands of friends and enemies alike. Do you really think scattered handfuls of people can prepare the ground for something so immense? I just don't know.

The repulsion I felt at the hell-bent pursuit of distinction around me was a sentimental perch for what I believed to be my democratic vision of vast processions of people in full rebellion—dreaming, vagabonding, and never giving in to the status quo. I once considered myself to be one of those people. I believed that since I was no better than all those who'd been crushed by the current storm, my personal failure was insignificant. I even believed I was quite lucky, thanks to the endless opportunity to pursue that thing called 'knowledge'.

But this way of seeing things began to fall apart as well about a year ago. I realize that poverty is eating away my soul and that I have to confront it methodically or else I'll be annihilated. I have to do this without the possible accusation of going back to what I call 'fascist thinking', or the old made-to-order categories and answers of the left. I feel the truth of every word I'm saying here very painfully. Why, tell me, do people always have to 'do' something to keep their souls from withering? Maybe I feel this way because my 'ordinary' life now is so empty. I've lost the ability to live simple, intimate relationships thanks to a past strewn with institutional obstacles and all sorts of competing interests. But if I actually *do* something, just to save my skin, am I not just going back to the same detestable point? (Someone whose intelligence you don't respect very much once said to me: The problem is that you want to do something you love but you don't love anything enough!). It's true that theory is my true forte but I do so hate 'the life of books'! I blame it for the tenuousness of my links to the real world as well as the fragility of my capacity to understand. I have absolutely no desire to do 'scientific research' or enter into the nit-picking and moribund battles of literary criticism in Egypt. If I have to 'do' something it has to be dynamic, pulsing with the life of the collective. That's why the idea of working in film crossed my mind—but I have so little technical knowledge. Dilettantism isn't the way to go I tell you.

I'm sorry this letter is so long, but at least now I've said everything I needed to say. Your patience has let me to see things I needed to see. But I still need your help because though I've managed to state the problem, I have no idea how to go about to solving it (it actually didn't occur to me when I started to write this letter that there even was a problem). One thing is clear though: if life won't open up a door that will let me connect to people in richer and more human ways, I have to make up my mind to build that door myself. Leaving Egypt just might help me to find the balance I need to be productive again (and maybe that's also an illusion). Until that moment comes, I have to start building—though what, I'm not exactly sure yet. I do know that it will all be meaningless if it's solitary work. In this lies the limit of my abilities.

Exact copy

Ishbiliya, June 1985

Dear [. . .]

I'm writing to you from Seville (Ishbiliya in Arabic) in the south of Spain, which is quite like Egypt's deep south. I've discovered that Seville is home to everything Spain is famed for the world over. It's a breathtakingly beautiful city. When I saw the river here, I couldn't help it, I got really homesick. It reminded of Egypt and of how it too has the potential to become a beautiful place one day.

I'm still quite alone, but the whole story of 'living with alienation' has taken a surprising and very serious turn. I'm no longer constantly at odds with it. On the contrary, I take pleasure in it now! It's more than just a feeling. I'm content with my solitude. My entire past, my whole store of experience is taking on a new shape; a new and maybe terminal position towards the world around me. I understand now that the bitter experience 'that killed me'—to rephrase the song from *An Egyptian Story*[1]—is basically the upshot of the brutal life we live in dead societies. (Isn't it strange how it can take your whole life to discover such a basic truth?). I was ambitious. I wanted to live a splendid and full existence, to escape from the deadening boredom of

1 [An iconic film by Yusuf Shahin that documents the cultural, social and political transformations in Egypt after 1952 through the 1980s.]

middle-class domesticity, but I was crushed at every turn. I suffered but I was also utterly bewildered. Why was I being abused when I never dreamt of hurting anyone? On the contrary, I only wanted to live in fuller harmony with people (I wasn't aware that this, above all else, was my Achilles' heel). But now I've accepted that 'escape' is impossible, just as it's impossible to create a utopia out of beauty and human intimacy in societies that are inhuman. It was right that life should mock my illusions because they were egotistical ones. I wanted to avoid the wretched destiny of the vast majority of people the world over, a destiny imposed on them with an iron fist by the minority of owners. I accept that life is a dirty business now. I don't believe in petty-bourgeois purity any more (they're the only class that lives in and through illusion, whether in the form of practised hypocrisy or permanent self-mortification). At the same time, I discovered why people call me 'cruel' even though I'm actually quite nice! It's because I despise the arrogance and coward-liness of 'purity' as an ethical imperative. The humil-iation I've suffered no longer makes me ashamed. There's nothing in my past that I'll deny, not even the long years of ideological blindness in all their narrow-mindedness and triviality. But I'm still not one of those so-called 'disillusioned' Marxists. I despise those people from the bottom of my heart. It's not that they were finally disabused of their fool's paradise; it's that they never knew what they were talking about in the first place. They never felt it or tried to live the truth of it. They never experienced the hardship of discovery. For them—those dogmatic friends with whom we wasted the most important years of our lives—Marxism was just an easy key to conquest.

I still believe deeply in the truth of Marxism. In art as in life, it's obscene to try to defend the ivory tower. That's the attitude of a class sated by death: the owners, enemies of life—may God damn them in every place—hell-bent on their own extinction and everyone else's! At the same time, I'm completely prepared to commit heresy and rethink Marxism from scratch. I'm done with the theological orthodoxy of the pseudo-communists whose ignorance of Marxism is equal to their ignorance of life. And by the way, if I were to ever get the chance to help come up with a party platform, I'd fight tooth and nail in order to set one condition for prospective members: a minimum age of 30 and a history of earning their bread by the sweat of their brow like the rest of God's creatures. Then we'd see who gets to play vanguard over whom.

In short, I've finally managed to achieve a kind of peace that I've been looking for from the moment I became conscious of the world around me. I can submit now to the power of life's logic, and it, in return, finally submits to me because I've paid the price and proved that I'm equal to the adventure I set out upon 19 years ago (imagine . . . I'm so old . . . 34 going on 40!).

On this note, I have to tell you that I've developed a sudden and very strange aversion to old people that sometimes borders on physical revulsion. They appear to me to be a kind of calumny on life. I'm reminded of something awful I once heard about a Japanese custom that when people get old, they pack up a very little bit of food, climb up to the top of a mountain and wait for death to take them. I can't help but think it might be a good idea really. I'm thinking that I might commit suicide when I get old. For the first time, I'm starting to contemplate the idea of death—not from a metaphysical perspective (the afterlife and so forth) but simply as an operation that ends life. I think I've begun to understand the idea a little and it seems to me that our notions of heroism are closely related to it. I think that heroism can never be anything other than an ordinary act, a piece of life as it is (taking into account everything about life that is extraordinary of course). It seems to me that the nature of a person's life is what determines the nature of their death. What does someone who is already emptied of life have to lose in death? Someone who's sick and forced to succumb to the humiliation of having his arse wiped by strangers, for example? In the room next door to me in the pension, there's a man like that. You have no idea how awful he is to me! If he were to die, at least he'd escape the slow and degrading effacement of his personality. I know what I'm saying sounds terribly cruel but, on top of everything else, there's no use in me lying. Death doesn't frighten me. I don't mean that I'd carelessly expose myself to danger—I love this world. What I mean is that at that moment when life loses its 'taste' for me, I think that I won't be afraid to die. And at the same time, I'd happily die for a cause. Then death would become an integral part of life (this phrase is so often repeated but I don't think most people really understand what it means). A person would be in a kind of state or moment in which the borders between his existence as an individual and the lives of others would vanish. This is why you'll rarely find an intellectual making this kind of sacrifice (forgive me—I do so hate intellectuals from the bottom of my heart). Looking at it this way, life is a unity, and you have to break off a piece to connect it to another piece. It's that simple. And if it wasn't that simple, it wouldn't have been possible for millions to do it every single day over the course of history. Whoever said the masses make history was right! Unfortunately, they make history by paying the price of making history alone. The thinking 'brain' is still monopolized by the intellectuals. It's only fair then that in spite of their monopoly of the achievements of the human mind, their souls are rotten—corpses tottering along on two feet. They have no idea how to take pleasure in life because they're so damn busy babbling about their experience and the only pain they know how to express takes the form of self-pity! As for all their talk about 'united action', to them it's really nothing but a kind of naivety! Even the ones who've never really lived claim to know everything. Aren't they great at playing God.

Exact copy

POSTSCRIPT
Violets Are Blue

How do you give joy, pretty violet
When you're such a sad flower.[1]

Allow me to dedicate this short postscript to the
dreamers—to the generation of the seventies. Their
dream of changing the world was a luxury denied to
later generations. Today's youth may be free of ideological blinders but the price they pay for this freedom
is almost complete surrender to the values of bourgeois society (and without even being conscious of this
surrender, without ever having experienced the light
of rebellion as we did). But we also paid an enormous
price for that short and thrilling moment. If we seem
to many of those who came before or after us to be
fallen angels, that's only because they believed in our
angelic nature—in the purity of our leftist kitsch—and
thereby gave us more credit than should be allowed to
any human being. These days the dreamers are no
longer wide-eyed stargazers (and perhaps never were)
but people permeated through and through by the
feculence their rebellion stirred up. The tragedy of a

[1] [A song from the Egyptian popular repertoire; lyrics by
Bayram al-Tunsi, composed by Riyad al-Sonbati and sung by
Salih Abd al-Hayy.]

generation that lived the experience of rebellion is that no matter where each individual ended up, whether they took the safe path (repentance, pragmatism, even repudiation of all the old radical ideas), or the path of remorse (emotional collapse, withdrawal from the world, mental illness) they can never go back to being the person they were before the rapture took them. They can never be free of the memory of that magnificent moment of transgression, of freedom; of a lightness whose beauty is almost unbearable. The dream will remain, as exhausting as compunction, as inspiring as the purest moments of exuberant life, and so painful. For the truth is that the 'road of no return' isn't just a third possible outcome. It's always there, at the very heart of the moment in which you stake your whole being in order to follow the dream. It's only later that you might settle down to the safe path or the sorry one. Rebellion is a moment of exception. It lit up every one of us with the purest light and also made us savage. And when the twisting road began to descend towards our terminus, the crudeness of what we had lived, of the things that we had done and that had been done to us, was now naked and visible for all to see. There was no 'historical context' to justify, or idealism to balance out any of it. All sorts of grievous wounds were quickly stitched up without being cleaned (the pain of confrontation was beyond endurance in many cases) and chronic infection thrived deep below the surfaces. This is the price that some of us continue to

pay till today, even in the most intimate of our relationships. We cannot escape the pain and we keep cir-
cling the crime scene, damned souls, despairing of
pardon.

And yet I can't help but wonder if all that's really
left of our old dream is a shattered illusion and a cache
of battle wounds. I'll say again that I don't think it's
possible to give anything but individual answers to this
question. For us, for our generation as a whole, there
is no answer. As far as I myself am concerned, I still
keep the possibility of dreaming close by, and this,
in spite of my growing suspicion that we are in fact
nearing the end of times. Marx was the last of the great
dreamers, and part of my brain will always tick with a
mechanism acquired from the world of his ideas. I
cannot but see the world and the people in it through
the prism of class relations. As for his critique of capitalist society, it is truer now than ever. The dream of
communist revolution was part of my expedition to
find and seize a kind of freedom I longed for but didn't
really understand. Perhaps I've found this freedom in
a way, for myself alone. That's not such a bad harvest.
At the same time, the emptiness and moral hypocrisy
of life in my country today is such that freedom is
obliged to hide inside the shells of shattered selves.